You & Yours

Lee Andersen

Lee is a New Zealander with a talented knitter for a mother.

She was brought up believing a house full of colourful yarn was normal and that knitting was just something that came off the needles. Her mother knitted whatever was necessary for the constantly accumulating children around her. (Lee is one of six and now there are grand children ...)

After completing a Bachelor of Education majoring in Art and a three year Diploma of Teaching, Lee began painting and exploring wearable art and, naturally, knitting surfaced as a medium.

When the designs started coming faster than her fingers could knit she began working with other knitters in New Zealand until over 100 of the best were working straight from her drawings.

Her gallery Vibrant Handknits in Wellington, New Zealand supplied "one only" garments to "the rich, the famous and the royal" from around the world for six years.

Then in 1988 Lee fell in love! Unfortunately, Al lived in a different country (the U.S.) and knitting needles and coloured pencils are mobile. Lee moved.

Her first book "You Knit, Unique" teaches knitters how to design and offers humourous but practical solutions to those inevitable mishaps.

This book belongs to a series of 20 pattern books for those knitters who want to knit a specific garment but still want suggestions for altering colour and sizes.

You & Yours

*Contemporary sweater designs for men
(and their female friends!)*

Lee Andersen

Vibrant Publishing
New Zealand

CONTENTS

Physical

Nature's Mountain

7

Strata

14

Soft Rock

18

Consistent Cables

23

Parking Lot

28

Saw Blade

34

Emotional

Paw Prints

39

How I Love Thee

44

Cubist Kiss

49

Gold Rock

56

Outlet

62

First published 1990
Vibrant Publishing
Box 17 257
New Zealand

CONTENTS

Intellectual

Side Bar
68

Corporate Spaces
74

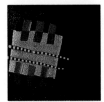
Computer Chips
80

Giant Cables
88

Silk Leaves
94

Spiritual

Santa Fe
98

Slash and Dash
103

Lightening
108

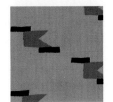
Art Deco
112

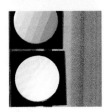
Invent
117

Leading the Eye	121
Sewing Up	126
Intarsia and Fairisle	126
Border Art	127
Acknowledgements	128

ISBN 0-908886-01-2

Introduction

There are two reasons for making a man a sweater.

The first is because you are a knit-aholic and he is a suitable recipient for the endless sweaters that flow off your needles. The second is because you are completely smitten with him

If you are a knit-aholic then husbands,children, next door neighbours and virtual strangers are all suitable recipients for sweaters. Boy children are especially useful because they grow and can be encouraged to be rough with their clothing and therefore need new sweaters all the time. True knit-aholics have to have a lot of husbands or a lot of children!

If you are of the smitten variety then you want the sweater to fit the smittee correctly. One of the major complaints from men is incorrect sizing. This is a secret desire to be hugged or measured around the chest, which is the same thing.

I use the hug method on my Al frequently so his sweaters always fit, but we have to negotiate on the third reason for knitting.

He complains that he never gets to wear HIS sweaters because I'm always wearing them. I do wear them. This is not unreasonable because women are more sensitive to the cold than men.

If you suspect you will be wearing them as much if not more than him then make the bands, neck and cuffs tighter. There is no such thing as a sweater which is too big in the body, and the firmer cuffs will make it practical for a smaller person to wear. If he complains that the cuffs are too tight then tell him ribbing will stretch in time so you are just being prudent.

Good luck with the negotiations. Personally I find truth in the phrase "possession is nine tenths of the law!"

All yarns in this book available from:

Eagle USA

P.O. Box 48282
Seattle, WA 98166
Fax: (206) 767-9768
Phone: (206) 767-9766

For substitute yarns please contact your local Eagle representative

Australia: contact Cleckheaton Yarns
New Zealand: contact Wendy Yarns

Finished garments available from Vibrant Handknits, Sue Graham, 74 Akaroa Road,
Maupuia, Wellington, New Zealand.

Nature's Mountain

Any mountain scene has a beauty and strength of its own. This one is recreated in natural coloured yarns with simple outlines in black. Three alternative colourways are provided at the end, including a more feminine version.

Yarns Required

A: UNIQUE l2 ply
    black 507 x 4
B: UNIQUE 12 ply
    cream 523 x 5
C: UNIQUE l2 ply
    grey 518 x 3
D: Cleckheaton NATURAL
    l2 ply cream 1030 x 4
E: Cleckheaton NATURAL
    l2 ply taupe 1034 x 2
F: Cleckheaton COLLAGE
    grey 1199 x 1
G: CHANSON
    patrol blue 925 X 1
H: Cleckheaton COLLAGE
    blue 1198 x l

Needles

5 mm (U.S.#7, U.K.#6)
    needles for the bands,
    cuff and neckband.
6 mm (U.S.#9, U.K.#4)
    needles for the body.

Tension or Gauge

stocking stitch (stockinette)
17 sts and 22 rows
to l0 cm (4 inches)

Garment Size

Width: 53 cm or 21" (58 cm
    or 23", 70 cm or 27¹/2")
Total stitches = 90 (100, 120)
Length: 60 cm or 23¹/2",
    (70 cm or 27¹/2")
Total rows = 132 (152)

Back Band

Cast on loosely 80 (90, 100) sts using the band needles in (A). Work the band for a total of 25 rows as follows:

Rib the first 7 rows in black. To do "Rib" knit 1, purl l, across the row. If you end with a knit stitch begin the next row with a purl.

Next front facing row: Keep the first 6 stitches in black rib. Add (C) and KNIT until the last 6 stitches. Tie on another ball of black and rib the last 6 stitches.

Continue RIBBING for the next 6 rows in (C) but keep the first and last 6 stitches in black. Cross over the yarns at the back to avoid holes. Work one row replacing (C) with (B). Continue ribbing

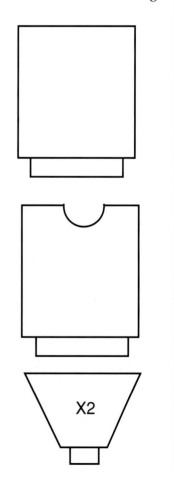

in (B) for 3 more rows.

Next front facing row: Return to all black. Rib the first and last 6 stitches and KNIT the black stitches inbetween. Rib the next 6 rows.

Back Body

Change to the body needles and do a purl row increasing to 90 (100, 120) sts evenly across the row. Begin the graph.

Reading a Graph

One stitch is represented by one square. Read from the bottom right hand corner to the left for the first knit row. Take special care for the first row because it establishes the position of all stitches above it.

Read from left to right for the purl row even though you will still be knitting from right to left. Turn the graph upside down if it helps.

Hint for Intarsia

When you join in each of the new colours tie a neat knot and leave 10 cm (4") tails. Weave these in behind each stitch at the back while that colour lasts on the graph then leave them till the next row if necessary. If the width of the new colour is too narrow to use this method leave the tail and sew it in later along the edge of the colour change.

Completing the back

There is no armhole shaping for a drop shoulder style and no neck shaping on the back. Fill in the neck hole on the back continuing in the basic design idea already established.

Cast off (bind off) straight across the last row maintaining the colours.

Front Band

As for the back.

Front

As for the back but this time shape the hole for the neck as shown on the graph.

26 rows from the end divide the two shoulders by putting the 20 central stitches on a stitch holder or a safety pin. This will make it easier to pick up for the neckband and will help make the neck elastic.

Decrease one stitch every 2nd row for 10 rows (five decreases in all). Continue straight for 16 rows.

Cast off, maintaining the colours.

Sleeve

Both sleeves are the same. Do not mirror image them. Cast on 35 stitches using the band needles. Work the band as for the bottom back band. Change to the body needles. Increase on a purl row evenly to 50 stitches using the body needles.

Use the central 50 stitches of the front graph but also increase one stitch each

edge every 4th row. The first part of the sleeve shaping is built into the design of the front to get you started.

Continue increasing every 4th row until the sleeve is long enough. Change the colours on the second sleeve if you wish but do not mirror image it.

When the sleeve is long enough cast off very loosely. The average sleeve will end after the 95th row of the graph.

Neck Band

Sew one shoulder seam using the Weaving method and using the matching colours. Use straight needles and make a seam or sew both shoulders and use round needles or four needles. Using a "band" needle like a crochet hook, (B) coloured yarn and facing the front of the work knit up stitches evenly around the hole as follows: 30 from the back of the neck, 13 along the straight vertical edge, 7 along the diagonal, knit the 20 from the safety pin to carry the yarn with you, then 7 and then 13. (Total= 90 stitches)

To avoid holes in the corners ignore that space and pick up stitches from either side of it. Rib for 25 rows.

Cast off (bind off) very loosely in rib using a "body" needle if necessary.

9

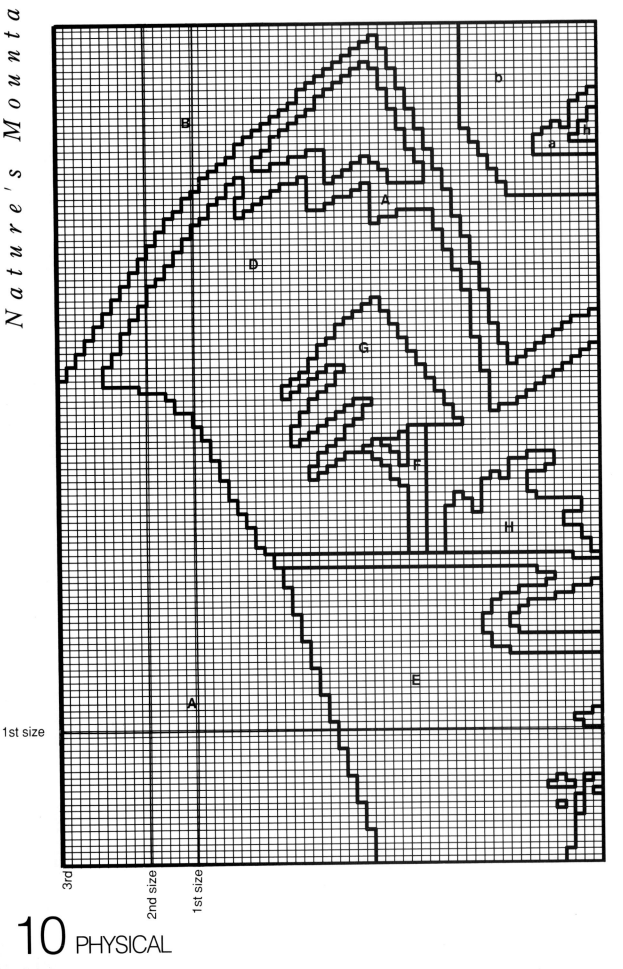

Sew the band seam using the Up through the Bar method and the remaining shoulder seam using the Weaving method. Fold the neckband inside. Sew each stitch down to its matching "picked up" stitch but make the loops slightly loose to allow the neck to stretch.

Sewing Up

This should be done from the outside using two different techniques: Weaving and Up through the Bar.

Sew the sleeve seams including the ribbed bands using the Up through the Bar method. Reinforce the beginning of the cuff.

Side seams

Use the Up through the Bar method for both the ribbed bands and the stocking stitch (stockinette) side seams. Begin at the band and reinforce the first few stitches. Sew up to within 28 cm (11") of the shoulder seams. Reinforce again.

Setting in the sleeves

Alternate every stitch using the Weaving method for the sleeve stitches and the Up through the Bar method for the body rows.

Five stitches from the sleeve will match seven rows from the body as for any drop shoulder garment.

Check the inside for any remaining tails and sew these in along the edges of the colour change using a large eyed needle.

Key Design Elements

The black drawn outlines evoke the simplicity and security of comic books and also the simple view of truth inherent in primitive art. Mountain imagery also has many positive, meditative associations.

Alternative Colourways

Always keep the black outline.

The original is in middle naturals. The basic feeling can be changed by shifting to: slates and blue-greys, or to coffee-browns and pale golds, or to silver greys and pale blues and white, or to deep rusts and plums and deep blue-greys.

Yarns Required
(For blue version)

A: UNIQUE 12 ply
   black 507 x 4

B: UNIQUE 12 ply
   lilac 513 x 5

C: UNIQUE 12 ply
   grey 518 x 3

D: COLLAGE
   blue 1198 x 4

E: COLLAGE 12 ply
   grey 1199 x 2

F: Cleckheaton NATURAL
   12 ply taupe 1034 x 2

G: CHANSON
   patrol blue 925 X 1

H: UNIQUE 12 ply
   cream 523 x 1

Yarns Required
(For rust version)

A: UNIQUE 12 ply
   black 507 x 4

B: UNIQUE 12 ply
   grey 518 x 5

C: Cleckheaton NATURAL
   12 ply taupe 1034 x 2

D: UNIQUE 12 ply
   purple 508 x 4

E: COLLAGE
   red 1208 x 2

F: Cleckheaton COLLAGE
   grey 1199 x 1

G: CHANSON
   patrol blue 925 X 1

H: Cleckheaton COLLAGE
   blue 1198 x 1

Yarns Required
(For female version)

A: CHANSON
   black 912 x 2 for bands
   and cuffs

A: MOHAIR 90
   ebony 885 x 2 for body

B: MOHAIR 90
   blue mist 879 x 3 for
   collar

C: MOHAIR 90
   enchanted forest 893 x 2

D: MOHAIR 90
   neptune 888 x 3

E: MOHAIR 90
   bewitched 892 x 2

or Eagle RENOIR
   green x 2

F: NOSTALGIA
   blue 1500 x 1

G: MOHAIR 90
   rose queen 878 x 1

13

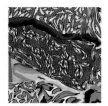

Strata

Excavated earthworks reveal both the deposits laid down and the effects of pressure and movement over time. Any rock face is a million sweater designs.

Yarns Required

A: UNIQUE 12 ply
    black 507 x 7
B: UNIQUE 12 ply
    cream 523 x 3
C: UNIQUE 12 ply
    gray 518 x 1
D: UNIQUE 12 ply
    camel 501 x 2
E: Cleckheaton
    NATURAL 12 ply
    grey 1031 x 2
F: Cleckheaton
    NATURAL 12 ply
    gold 1013 x 1
G: Cleckheaton COLLAGE
    grey 1199 x 4
H: Cleckheaton SENSATION
    black 1271 x 2

Needles

5 mm (U.S.#7, U.K.#6)
    needles for the bands,
    cuff and neckband.
6 mm (U.S.#9, U.K.#4)
    needles for the body.

Tension or Gauge

stocking stitch (stockinette)
17 sts and 22 rows
to l0 cm (4 inches)

Garment Size

Width: 53 cm or 21" (58 cm
    or 23", 70 cm or 27^1/$_2$")
Total stitches = 90 (100, 120)
Length: 60 cm or 23^1/$_2$",
    (70 cm or 27^1/$_2$".)
Total rows = 132 (152)

Back Band

Cast on loosely 80 (90, 100)
sts using the band needles
in black. Work the band for
a total of 25 rows as follows:

Rib the first 7 rows in black.
To do "Rib" knit 1, purl l,
across the row. If you end
with a knit stitch begin the
next row with a purl.

Next front facing row: Keep
the first 6 stitches in black
rib but then add (G) and
KNIT until the last 6
stitches. Tie on another ball
of black and rib the last 6
stitches.

Continue RIBBING for the
next 9 rows in (G) but keep
the first and last 6 stitches in
black. Cross over the yarns
at the back to avoid holes.

Next front facing row:
Return to all black. Rib the

first and last 6 stitches and
KNIT the black stitches
inbetween. Rib the next 6
rows in black.

Back Body

Change to the body needles
and do a purl row
increasing to 90 (100, 120)
sts evenly across the row.
Begin the graph.

Reading a Graph

One stitch is represented by
one square. Read from the

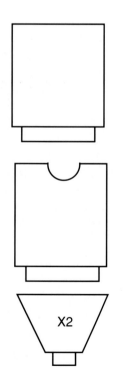

15

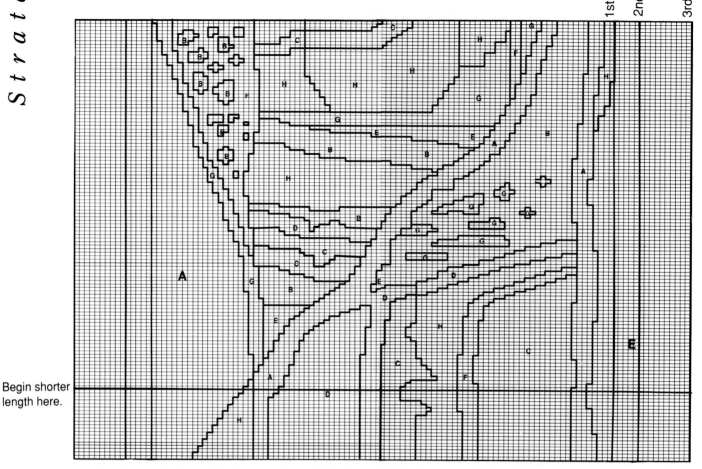

Begin shorter
length here.

bottom right hand corner to
the left for the first knit row.
Take special care for the
first row because it
establishes the position of
all stitches above it.

Read from left to right for
the purl row even though
you will still be knitting
from right to left. Turn the
graph upside down if it
helps.

Hint for Intarsia
When you join in each of
the new colours tie a neat
knot and leave 10 cm (4")
tails. Weave these in behind
each stitch at the back while
that colour lasts on the
graph then leave them till
the next row if necessary. If
the width of the new colour
is too narrow to use this
method leave the tail and

sew it in later along the
edge of the colour change.

Completing the back
There is no armhole shaping
for a drop shoulder style
and no neck shaping on the
back. Fill in the neck hole on
the back, as indicated on the
graph. Cast off (bind off)
straight across the last row
maintaining the colours.

Front Band
As for the back.

Front
As for the back but this time
shape the hole for the neck
as shown on the graph.

26 rows from the end divide
the two shoulders by
putting the 20 central
stitches on a stitch holder or
a safety pin. This will make

it easier to pick up for the
neckband and will help
make the neck elastic.
Decrease one stitch every
2nd row for 10 rows (five
decreases in all). Continue
straight for 16 rows. Cast off
maintaining the colours.

Sleeve
Both sleeves are the same.
Do not mirror image them.
Cast on 35 stitches using the
band needles. Work the
band as for the bottom back
band. Change to the body
needles. Increase on a purl
row evenly to 50 stitches
using the body needles.

Use the central 50 stitches of
the front graph but also
increase one stitch each
edge every 4th row.
Continue increasing every
4th row until the sleeve is

long enough. Change the colours on the second sleeve if you wish but do not mirror image it.

When the sleeve is long enough cast off very loosely. The average sleeve will end after the 95th row of the graph.

Neck Band

Sew one shoulder seam using the Weaving method and using the matching colours. Use straight needles and make a seam or sew both shoulders and use round needles or four needles.

Using a "band" needle like a crochet hook, black yarn and facing the front of the work knit up stitches evenly around the hole as follows: 30 from the back of the neck, 13 along the straight vertical edge, 7 along the diagonal, knit the 20 from the safety pin to carry the yarn with you, then 7 and then 13. (Total= 90 stitches) To avoid holes in the corners ignore that space and pick up stitches from either side of it.

Rib in black for 7 rows, change to (G) and KNIT the first front facing row. Continue ribbing in (G) for 5 rows and then go back to black KNITTING the first row. Continue ribbing in black for a further 23 rows. Cast off (bind off) loosely in rib using a "body" needle if necessary. Sew the band seam using the Up through

the Bar method and the remaining shoulder seam using the Weaving method.

Fold the neckband inside. Sew each stitch down to its matching "picked up" stitch but make the loops slightly loose to allow the neck to stretch.

Sewing Up

This should be done from the outside using two different techniques: Weaving and Up through the Bar.

Sew the sleeve seams including the ribbed bands using the Up through the Bar method. Reinforce the beginning of the cuff.

Side seams

Use the Up through the Bar method for both the ribbed bands and the stocking stitch (stockinette) side seams. Begin at the band and reinforce the first few stitches. Sew up to 28 cm or 11" from the shoulder seams. Reinforce again.

Setting in the sleeves

Alternate every stitch using the Weaving method for the sleeve stitches and the Up through the Bar method for the body rows.

Five stitches from the sleeve will match seven rows from the body as for any drop shoulder garment.

Check the inside for any remaining tails and sew these in along the edges of

the colour change using a large eyed needle.

Alternative Colourways

The original is in middle earth colours with a tendency towards natural sheep grey. Alternatives are as varied as the earth itself.

This is an ideal design to work with handspun yarns. Keep the black as black or a very dark charcoal to give the design its structure but play with the colours of each divided area.

Try plums, browns and purples or lilacs, greys and white or coffee, greys and honey or slate blues, blues and grey.

Small areas of turquoise and terra cotta added to a gold, brown and black combination will give a South Western look.

Keep large areas of light colours up on the chest and shoulders and away from the hips and tummy.

This design is also suitable for bright primary and secondary colours. Keep the yellow and oranges up towards the chest and off the hips.

Key Design Elements

The general balance of the 'division of area' and the predominantly dark sides are the stable elements in this design. The range from black to cream is extreme and offers drama.

17

Soft Rock

Sedimentary rock under pressure waves like the sea. This design is a formalised version of that process. The colours repeat and are spaced for balance.

Yarns Required

A: UNIQUE 12 ply
   black 507 x 6
B: UNIQUE 12 ply
   gray 518 x 6
C: Cleckheaton COLLAGE
   grey 1199 x 6
D: Cleckheaton
   SENSATION
   black 1271 x 6
E: UNIQUE 12 ply
   white 503 x 2

Needles

5 mm (U.S.#7, U.K.#6)
   needles for the bands,
   cuff and neckband.
6 mm (U.S.#9, U.K.#4)
   needles for the body.

Tension or Gauge

stocking stitch (stockinette)
   17 sts and 22 rows
   to l0 cm (4 inches)

Garment Size

Width: 53 cm or 21" (58 cm
   or 23", 70 cm or 27^1/2")
Total stitches = 90 (100, 120)
Length: 60 cm or 23^1/2" (70
   cm or 27^1/2")
Total rows = 132 (152)

Back

Cast on loosely 80 (90, 100) sts using the band needles and black. Work the band for a total of 25 rows in ribbing.

Change to the body needles and do a purl row increasing to 90 (100, 120) sts evenly across the row. Begin the graph.

Reading a Graph

One stitch is represented by one square. Read from the bottom right hand corner to the left for the first knit row. Take special care for the first row because it establishes the position of all stitches above it.

Read from left to right for the purl row even though you will still be knitting from right to left. Turn the graph upside down if it helps.

Hint for Intarsia

 When you join in each of the new colours tie a neat knot and leave 10 cm (4") tails. Weave these in behind each stitch at the back while that colour lasts on the graph then leave them till the next row if necessary. If the width of the new colour is too narrow to use this method leave the tail and sew it in later along the edge of the colour change.

Completing the back

There is no armhole shaping for a drop shoulder style and no neck shaping on the back. Fill in the neck hole on the back continuing in the basic design idea already established.

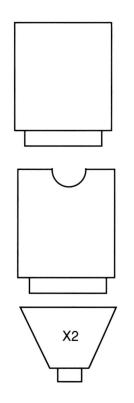

19

Cast off (bind off) straight across the last row maintaining the colours.

Front

As for the back but this time shape the hole for the neck as shown on the graph.

26 rows from the end divide the two shoulders by putting the 20 central stitches on a stitch holder or a safety pin. This will make it easier to pick up for the neckband and will help make the neck elastic. Decrease one stitch every 2nd row for 10 rows (five decreases in all). Continue straight for 16 rows. Cast off maintaining the colours.

Sleeve

Both sleeves are the same. Do not mirror image them. Cast on 35 stitches using the band needles. Work the band as for the bottom back band. Change to the body needles. Increase on a purl row evenly to 50 stitches using the body needles.

Use the central 50 stitches of the front graph but also increase one stitch each edge every 4th row. Continue increasing every 4th row until the sleeve is long enough. Change the position of the colours on the second sleeve if you wish but do not mirror image it.

When the sleeve is long enough cast off very loosely. The average sleeve will end after the 95th row of the graph.

Neck Band

Sew one shoulder seam using the Weaving method and using the matching colours. Use straight needles and make a seam or sew both shoulders and use round needles or four needles. Using a "band" needle like a crochet hook, black yarn, and facing the front of the work knit up stitches evenly around the hole as follows: 30 from the back of the neck, 13 along the straight vertical edge, 7 along the diagonal, knit the 20 from the safety pin to carry the yarn with you, then 7 and then 13. (Total= 90 stitches)

To avoid holes in the corners ignore that space and pick up stitches from either side of it. Rib for 25 rows. Cast off (bind off) very loosely in rib using a "body" needle if necessary. Sew the band seam using the Up through the Bar method and the remaining shoulder seam using the Weaving method.

Fold the neckband inside. Sew each stitch down to its matching "picked up" stitch but make the loops slightly loose to allow the neck to stretch.

Sewing Up

This should be done from the outside using two different techniques: Weaving and Up through the Bar.

Sew the sleeve seams including the ribbed bands using the Up through the Bar method. Reinforce the beginning of the cuff as this will be under a lot of stress over the years.

Sew the shoulder seams first if this is not already done using the Weaving method loosely.

Side seams

Use the Up through the Bar method for both the ribbed bands and the stocking stitch (stockinette) side seams. Begin at the band and reinforce the first few stitches. Sew up to within 28 cms (11") from the shoulder seams. Reinforce again.

Setting in the sleeves

Alternate every stitch using the Weaving method for the sleeve stitches and the Up through the Bar method for the body rows.

Five stitches from the sleeve will match seven rows from the body as for any drop shoulder garment.

Check the inside for any remaining tails and sew these in along the edges of the colour change using a large eyed needle.

Alternative Colourways

This design is very adaptable.

The original is in black and white and greys.

The SENSATION in this

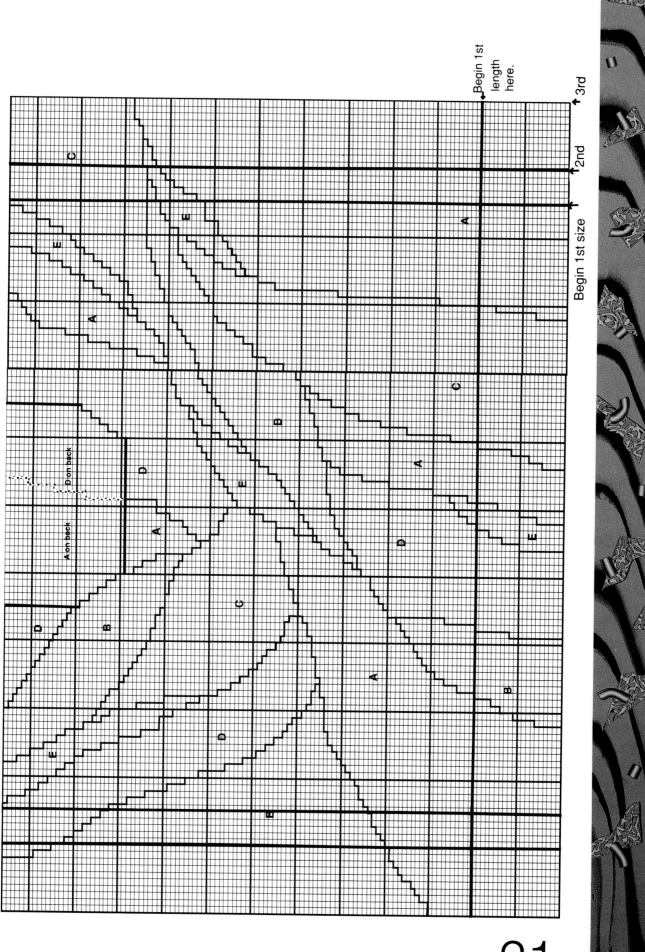

Begin 1st length here.

3rd

2nd

Begin 1st size

C

E

E

A

A

C

B

D

D on back

D

A

E

A on back

A

D

C

E

D

B

A

B

D

E

E

D

21

and silver thread 880, saucy mint 881 MOHAIR 90 and lilac KASHMIR MOHAIR 1692..

Try it in perfect blue 890, ebony black, neptune 888 MOHAIR 90 and NOSTALGIA purple 1503.

Try it in mother of pearl 886, cool caramel 883, truffle chantale 884 and ebony black MOHAIR 90.

When choosing colours think in terms of related colours. Keep them all bright, or all muddy, or all greyed, or all pastel. Position the "different" colour in the group where the white appears in the original. This area is always smaller than the others, therefore, it can handle stronger, brighter or more textured yarns and still maintain the balance.

For extra fun work with hairy eyelash yarns, metallics or heavily textured stitch types in the "white" position.

Hold odd colours together if you are working with scrap yarn by outlining in black.

Key Design Elements

The soft waves are all equally spaced and of similar size and curvature and so the colour choice becomes the key.

The repetition of the same colours over the whole garment is reassuring.

design can be changed to any other colour SENSATION and it will still work. Keep the black and white but use a co-ordinating colour of UNIQUE.

With red Sensation, use purple UNIQUE 508 or gold UNIQUE 504.

With blue Sensation, use princess blue UNIQUE 510.

With green Sensation, use lilac UNIQUE 513, or saxe blue UNIQUE 521.

With purple Sensation, use nut brown UNIQUE 520, or purple UNIQUE 508.

With navy Sensation, use red UNIQUE 514, camel UNIQUE 501 or princess UNIQUE 510.

For a completely different feel try all bright colours or all soft colours in MOHAIR 90.

Try it in neptune 888, crimson lake 891 and bewitched purple 892 MOHAIR 90 with hot pink NOSTALGIA 1502.

Try it in perfect blue 890, neptune 888, enchanted forest 893 MOHAIR 90 and Eagle RENOIR green.

Try it in rose queen pink 878

Consistent Cables

Lifes little rough patches and the constantly changing environment will not stop these "consistent cables" from travelling up the garment. The random blocks of colour and random textured stitches and yarns can be placed anywhere you like. Try to keep yarns which are thicker or thinner than average in small areas, but otherwise, just play.

Yarns Required

A: UNIQUE
   8 ply cream 423 x 9
B: UNIQUE
   8 ply gray 418 x 5
C: Cleckheaton
   HIGHLAND
   grey 1129 x 4
D: UNIQUE
   8 ply white 403 x 1
E: Cleckheaton NATURAL
   12 ply grey 1031 x 3
F: Cleckheaton NATURAL
   12 ply taupe 1034 x 2
G: Cleckheaton NATURAL
   12 ply cream 1030 x 1
H: Any DK or 8 ply
   grey and taupe cotton
   used together x 1 or any
   neutral mix
I: Cleckheaton NATURAL
   charcoal 1032 x 1
J: Cleckheaton HIGHLAND
   blue grey 1149 x 1
K: ANGORA SUPREME
   camel 1361 x 1

L: Cleckheaton HIGHLAND
   light grey 1129 x 1
M: Plus 50 gms of any extra
   fun, silky, lumpy bits!

Needles

3.5 mm (U.S.#4, U.K.#10)
   needles for the bands,
   cuff and neckband.
4 mm (U.S.#6, U.K.#8)
   needles for the body.

Tension or Gauge

stocking stitch (stockinette)
22 sts and 30 rows
to 10 cm (4 inches)

Garment Size

Body Width: 50 cms or
   19^1/2" (60 cm or 23^1/2"
   70 cm or 27^1/2")
Stitch numbers = 134 (156,
   178)
Total Length: 60 cm or
   23^1/2" (65 cm or 25 ^{1}/2",
   70 cm or 27 ^{1}/2")

Row numbers = 180 (195,
   210)
Any combinations may be
made depending on your
needs. The graph is for the
smallest size.

To increase the width

Halve the extra stitches that
you need and add them

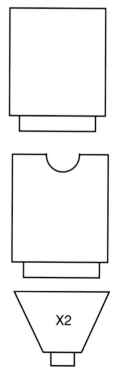

onto either side of the graph. Work these extra sts in squares. Use yarns in a similar colour range and texture but keep them 'darkish' and 'flattish.'

Back

Using (A) cast on loosely 100 (120, 140) sts using the band needles. Work the band in rib for 25 rows.

Change to the body needles and do a purl row increasing to 110 (132, 154) sts evenly across the row.

Knit the next row. Put a marker after the 22nd stitch, the 30th stitch, the 51st stitch, the 59th stitch, the 80th stitch and the 88th stitch.

The 8 stitch spaces mark the positions of the cables but they also need extra stitches to allow for the crossing over process.

Purl the next row working twice into every one of the three sets of eight cable stitches. Total = 134 (156, 178)

Change to body needles.

You are now ready to begin the graph in stocking stitch (stockinette) or in a range of textured stitches as in our model.

Make up your own textured stitches. A reverse stocking stitch is a good basic texture for an interesting yarn. Moss (or seed) or any

random knit purl stitch will work.

Read the graph beginning from the bottom right corner and read left for the first row and right for the second. You may find it easier to tip the graph upside down to read every second row if you are not very experienced.

Use a separate ball every time a new colour appears.

Hint for Intarsia

When you join in each of the new colours tie a neat knot and leave 10 cm (4") tails. Weave these in each stitch at the back while that colour lasts on the graph then leave them till the next row if necessary. If the width of the new colour is too narrow to use this method leave the tail and sew it in later along the edge of the colour change.

Cable pattern

ROW 1: Maintain the block design but also work the three cables across the body as follows: work 20 (31, 42) sts.

Right cable: P 2, K 4, put 2 onto a cable needle and hold to the back, K 2, K 2 off the cable needle , put the next 2 onto a cable needle, K 4, P 2.

Work 19 sts and then work the central cable as the right cable, work 19 sts and cable as right cable, work remaining 20 (31, 42) sts.

ROW 2: Purl while maintaining block design.

ROW 3: Continue block design introducing any other textured sts as desired but work cable as follows: P 2, K 2, put 2 onto cable needle and hold to back , K 2, K the 2 off the needle, put the next 2 onto a cable needle, K 2, K the 2 off the needle, K 2, P 2.

ROW 4: Work the blocks as desired but work the cable sts as follows:

Knit the knit sts and purl the purl sts.

ROW 5: As above but cable as follows: P 2, put 2 onto the cable needle and hold to the back, K 2, K the 2 off the needle, K 8, put the next 2 onto the cable needle, K 2, knit the 2 off the cable needle, P 2.

ROW 6: as row 4.

Repeat from row 1.

There is no armhole shaping for a drop shoulder style and no neck shaping on the back so continue the graph filling in the hole for the front neck shaping.

Cast off (bind off) straight across the last row loosely so the shoulders will stretch comfortably.

Front

As for the back but this time shape the hole for the neck as indicated on the graph.

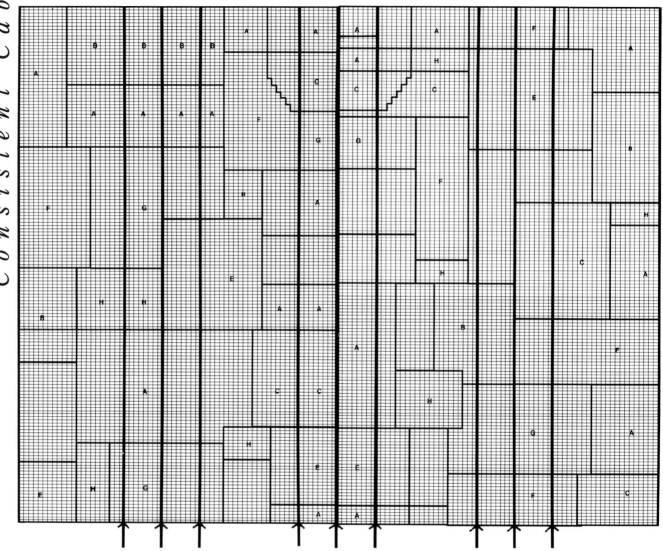

Divide the two shoulders by putting the 20 central stitches on a stitch holder or a safety pin. This will make it easier to pick up for the neckband and will help make the neck elastic. Decrease one each side every row for 10 rows.

Continue straight for 22 rows. Cast off loosely.

Sleeve

The sleeves do not need to be the same colours and textured stitches.

Cast on loosely 40 sts using the band needles and band yarn. Rib as for bottom band.

Increase on a purl row to 50 sts. Mark the central 8 sts on a knit row. On a purl row work into each of the cable stitches twice. Total = 58 sts.

Begin the sleeve using the body graph. The central cable of the sleeve is also the central cable of the body. Continue as for the body

but also increase one stitch each edge every 4th row. Begin working the other cables as the increase in stitches allows if you wish. When the sleeve is long enough cast off very loosely. The average sleeve is 50 cms in length.

Neck Band

Sew one shoulder seam using the Weaving method. Use straight needles and make a seam or sew both shoulders and use round needles or four needles.

Using a "band" needle like a crochet hook and the band yarn (A) or the yarn which matches the top of the garment, face the front of the work and knit up stitches evenly around the hole as follows:

30 from the back of the neck, 18 along the straight vertical edge, 13 along the diagonal, knit the 20 from the safety pin to carry the yarn with you, then 13 and then 18. (Total=112 stitches) To avoid holes in the corners ignore that space and pick up stitches from either side of it.

Rib as for the band but also continue to work the cable from the central cable on the body for the first 16 rows.

Cast off (bind off) very loosely in rib.

Sew the remaining shoulder seam. Sew the neck band seam using the Up through the Bar method.

To Make Up
This should be done from the outside using two different techniques: Weaving and Up through the Bar.

Sew the sleeve seams including the ribbed bands using the Up through the Bar method. Reinforce the beginning of the cuff. Sew the remaining shoulder seam.

Lay the garment flat and find the armpit by stretching the cast off (bind off) row of the sleeve as deep as possible (at least 28 cms or 11 inches from the shoulder seam.) Tie the front to the back at this point on both sides of the body.

Side seams
Use the Up through the Bar method for both the ribbed bands and the stocking stitch (stockinette) side seams. Begin at the band and reinforce the first few stitches. Sew up to the ties at the arm pits. Reinforce again.

Setting in the sleeves
Alternate every stitch using the Weaving method for the sleeve stitches and the Up through the Bar method for the body rows.

Five stitches from the sleeve will match seven rows from the body as for any drop shoulder garment.

Check the inside for any remaining tails and sew these in along the edges of the colour change using a large eyed needle.

Alternative Colourways
The original moves from black to cream via greys and naturals.

Alternatives would be: black to red, via browns and plums

black to blue, via forest greens and purples

black to gold, via purples and reds.

If you prefer a less patchy look to the colours then choose colours which are close to each other. A good way of selecting from your yarn collection is to try the "photo test." Imagine taking a black and white photo of all your yarns. Two "close" yarns would become the same grey in your photograph.

To skip the photo test stage, train your eye to see this same relationship by squinting at all your yarns. This tends to reduce the importance of the colour and let your eye focus on the similarities of tone that you are looking for.

Remember, if you want to flatter the physique (or figure) then work with predominantly darker, cooler colours at the bottom and gradually introduce more of the creams and whites up towards the shoulders. This will lead the eye up to the chest and shoulders and also make them look bigger.

Key Design Elements
The cables run "consistently" through changing yarns and textures. This contrast in purpose between the cables and the blocks is the key.

The cables themselves are not obvious, graphically, but they are symbolic.

27

Parking Lot

This design is from an aerial view of a parking lot with its strong simple diagonals. Extra diagonal zig zags are added to increase the energy level. Using mohair dresses up this design for 'after five' wear.

Yarns Required
A: MOHAIR 90
    ebony 885 x 2
B: MOHAIR 90
    mother of pearl 886 x 9

Needles
5 mm (U.S.#7, U.K.#6)
    needles for the bands,
    cuff and neckband.
6 mm (U.S.#9, U.K.#4)
    needles for the body.

Tension or Gauge
stocking stitch (stockinette)
17 sts and 22 rows
to l0 cm (4 inches)

Garment size
Width: 53 cm or 21" (58 cm
    or 23", 70 cm or 27¹/2")
Total stitches = 90 (100, 120)
Length: 60 cms or 23¹/2",
    (70 cm or 27¹/2")
Total rows = 132 (152)

Back Band
Cast on loosely 80 (90, 100)
sts using the band needles in (A). Work the band for a total of 22 rows as follows:

Rib the first 6 rows in black. To do "Rib" knit 1, purl l, across the row. If you end with a knit stitch begin the next row with a purl.

Next front facing row: Keep the first 6 stitches in black rib then add (B) and KNIT until the last 6 stitches. Tie on another ball of black and rib the last 6 stitches.

Continue RIBBING for the next 10 rows in (B)) but keep the first and last 6 stitches in black. Cross over the yarns at the back to avoid holes.

Next front facing row: return to all black. Rib the first and last 6 stitches and KNIT the black stitches inbetween. Rib the next 6 rows.

Back Body
Change to the body needles and do a purl row increasing to 90 (100, 120) sts evenly across the row. Begin the graph.

Reading a Graph
One stitch is represented by one square. Read from the bottom right hand corner to the left for the first knit row. Take special care for the first row because it

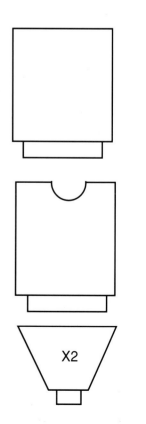

29

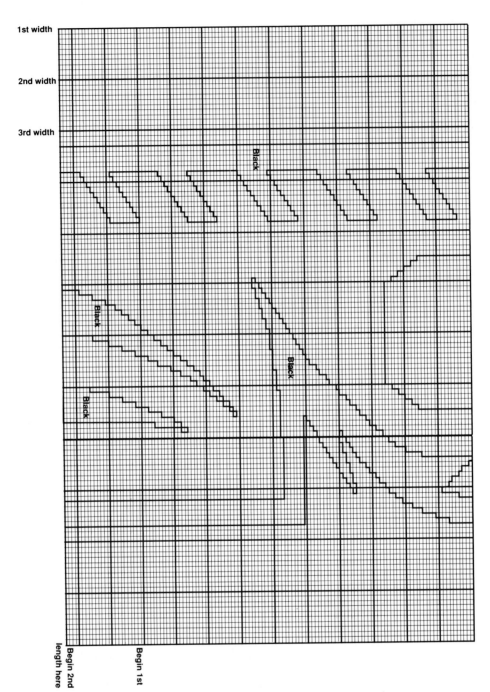

1st width

2nd width

3rd width

Black

Black

Black

Black

Begin 2nd length here

Begin 1st

establishes the position of all stitches above it.

Read from left to right for the purl row even though you will still be knitting from right to left. Turn the graph upside down if it helps.

Hint for Intarsia
Work with a separate ball of black and a separate ball of (B) every time it appears across the row for the first time. When you join in each of the new yarns tie a neat knot and leave 10 cm (4 ") tails. Weave these in behind each stitch at the back while that colour lasts on the graph then leave them till the next row if necessary. If the width of the new colour is too narrow to use this method leave the tail and sew it in later along the edge of the colour change.

Do not try to carry the black in behind the other colour.

Completing the back
There is no armhole shaping for a drop shoulder style and no neck shaping on the back. Fill in the neck hole on the back as indicated on the graph.

Cast off (bind off) straight across the last row maintaining the colours.

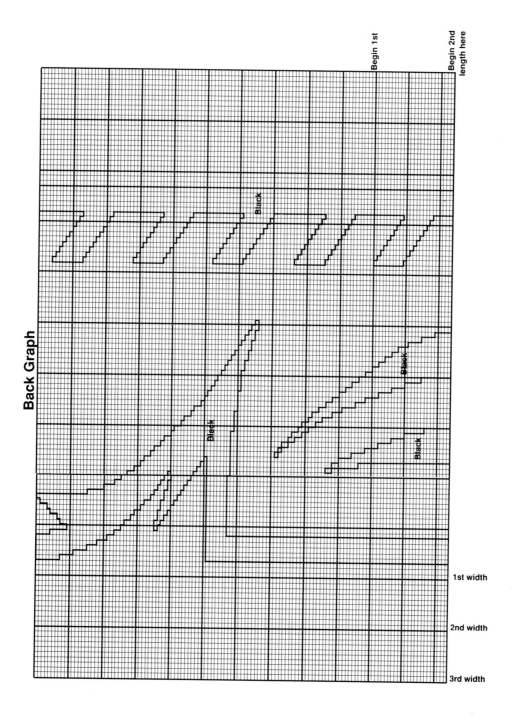

Back Graph

Black

Black

Black

Black

1st width

2nd width

3rd width

Front Band
As for the back.

Front
As for the back but this time shape the hole for the neck as shown on the graph.

26 rows from the end divide the two shoulders by putting the 20 central stitches on a stitch holder or a safety pin. This will make it easier to pick up for the neckband and will help make the neck elastic. Decrease one stitch every 2nd row for 10 rows (five decreases in all). Continue straight for 16 rows. Cast off maintaining the colours.

Sleeve
Both sleeves are the same. Do not mirror image them. Cast on 35 stitches using the band needles. Work the band as for the bottom back band. Change to the body needles. Increase on a purl row evenly to 50 stitches using the body needles.

Use the graph and increase one stitch each edge every 4th row. Continue increasing every 4th row until the sleeve is long enough.

When the sleeve is long enough cast off very loosely.

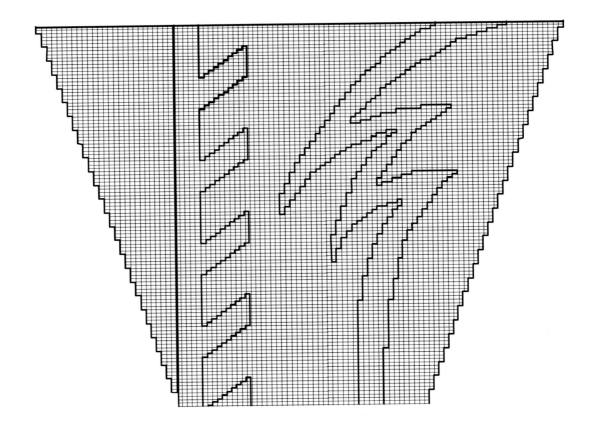

The average sleeve will end after the 95th row of the graph.

Neck Band

Sew one shoulder seam using the Weaving method and using the matching colours. Use straight needles and make a seam or sew both shoulders and use round needles or four needles.

Using a "band" needle like a crochet hook, black yarn and facing the front of the work knit up stitches evenly around the hole as follows: 30 from the back of the neck,13 along the straight vertical edge, 7 along the diagonal, knit the 20 from the safety pin to carry the yarn with you, then 7 and then 13. (Total= 90 stitches)

To avoid holes in the corners ignore that space and pick up stitches from either side of it.

Rib for 6 rows.

Change to (B) and KNIT the first (front facing) row. Continue ribbing for 6 rows and then change back to black. KNIT the first (front facing) row.

Rib for 8 more rows in black.

Cast off (bind off) loosely in rib using a "body" needle if necessary.

Sew the band seam using the Up through the Bar method and the remaining shoulder seam using the Weaving method. Fold the black at the top of the neckband inside.

 Sew each stitch down to the matching stitch at the beginning of the black to make a small roll. Stitch 1oosely to allow the neck to stretch.

Sewing Up

This should be done from the outside using two different techniques: Weaving and Up through the Bar.

Sew the sleeve seams including the ribbed bands using the Up through the Bar method. Reinforce the beginning of the cuff.

Side seams

Use the Up through the Bar method for both the ribbed

bands and the stocking stitch (stockinette) side seams. Begin at the band and reinforce the first few stitches. Sew up to within 28 cms (11") of the shoulder seam. Reinforce again.

Setting in the sleeves

Alternate every stitch using the Weaving method for the sleeve stitches and the Up through the Bar method for the body rows.

Five stitches from the sleeve will match seven rows from the body as for any drop shoulder garment.

Check the inside for any remaining tails and sew these in along the edges of the colour change using a large eyed needle.

Alternative Colourways

The original is in black and cream but any two colours may be used.

It also adapts to a more feminine look by softening the colours.

Alternatives are:

Yarns Required

A: MOHAIR 90
   ebony 885 x 2
B: MOHAIR 90
   neptune 888 x 9

Yarns Required

A: MOHAIR 90
   ebony 885 x 2
B: MOHAIR 90
   bewitched purple 892 x 9

Yarns Required

A: MOHAIR 90
   ebony 885 x 2
B: MOHAIR 90
   crimson lake 891 x 9

Yarns Required

A: MOHAIR 90
   ebony 885 x 2
B: MOHAIR 90
   silver thread 880 x 9

Yarns Required

A: MOHAIR 90
   ebony 885 x 2
B: MOHAIR 90
   truffle chantale 884 x 9

Yarns Required

A: MOHAIR 90
   ebony 885 x 2
B: MOHAIR 90
   perfect blue 890 x 9

Yarns Required

A: MOHAIR 90
   ebony 885 x 2
B: MOHAIR 90
   rose queen 878 x 9

If wool is prefered to mohair use the 12 ply UNIQUE and the stitch numbers will still work. Cleckheaton COLLAGE colours will also substitute.

Yarns Required

A: UNIQUE 12 ply
   black 507 x 2
B: UNIQUE 12 ply
   camel 501 x 9

Yarns Required

A: UNIQUE 12 ply
   black 507 x 2
B: UNIQUE 12 ply
   saxe blue 521 x 9

Yarns Required

A: UNIQUE 12 ply
   black 507x 2
B: UNIQUE 12 ply
   red 514 x 9

Yarns Required

A: UNIQUE 12 ply
   black 507 x 2
B: UNIQUE 12 ply
   lilac 513 x 9

Yarns Required

A: UNIQUE 12 ply
   black 507 x 2
B: UNIQUE 12 ply
   Cleckheaton COLLAGE
   blue 1198 x 9

Key Design Elements

The strong contrast and active relationship between the black lines and the spaces in the background is the key.

Saw Blade

Simple diagonals cut the space into triangular areas which zig zag in opposing directions. The colours work from dark up to light over the shoulders to make the shoulders look bigger than the hips.

Yarns Required
(Male)
A: UNIQUE 8 ply
    navy 409 x 4

B: UNIQUE 8 ply
    petral 411 x 3

C: UNIQUE 8 ply
    spruce 402 x 3

D: UNIQUE 8 ply
    gray 418 x 2

E: UNIQUE 8 ply
    lilac 413 x 1

Yarns Required
(Female)
A: UNIQUE 8 ply
    nut brown 420 x 4

B: UNIQUE 8 ply
    brick red 406 x 3

C: UNIQUE 8 ply
    gold 404 x 3

D: UNIQUE 8 ply
    cream 423 x 2

E: UNIQUE 8 ply
    brick red 406 x 1

Needles
3.5 mm (U.S.#4 U.K.#10)
    needles for the bands,
    cuff and neckband.

4 mm (U.S.#6, U.K.#8)
    needles for the body.

Tension or Gauge
stocking stitch (stockinette)
22 sts and 30 rows
to 10 cm (4 inches)

Garment Size
Body Width: 50 cm or
    $19^1/2$" (60 cm or $23^1/2$",
    70 cm or $27^1/2$")

Stitch numbers = 110 (132,
    154)

Total Length: 60 cms or
    $23^1/2$" (65 cm or $25^1/2$",
    70 cm or $27^1/2$")

Row numbers = 180 (195,
    210)

The graph shows the
smallest size.

To increase the width
Halve the extra stitches that
you need and add them
onto either side of the
graph. Work the extra
stitches in the main
background colour on that
side.

Back
Cast on loosely 100 (120,
140) sts using the band
needles. Work the band in
rib for 25 rows.

Change to the body needles
and do a purl row
increasing to 110 (132, 154)
sts evenly across the row.

You are now ready to begin
the graph in stocking stitch
(stockinette.)

Read the graph beginning
from the bottom right
corner and read left for the
first row and right for the
second. You may find it
easier to tip the graph
upside down to read every
second row.

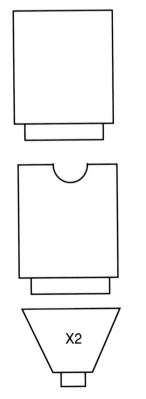

35

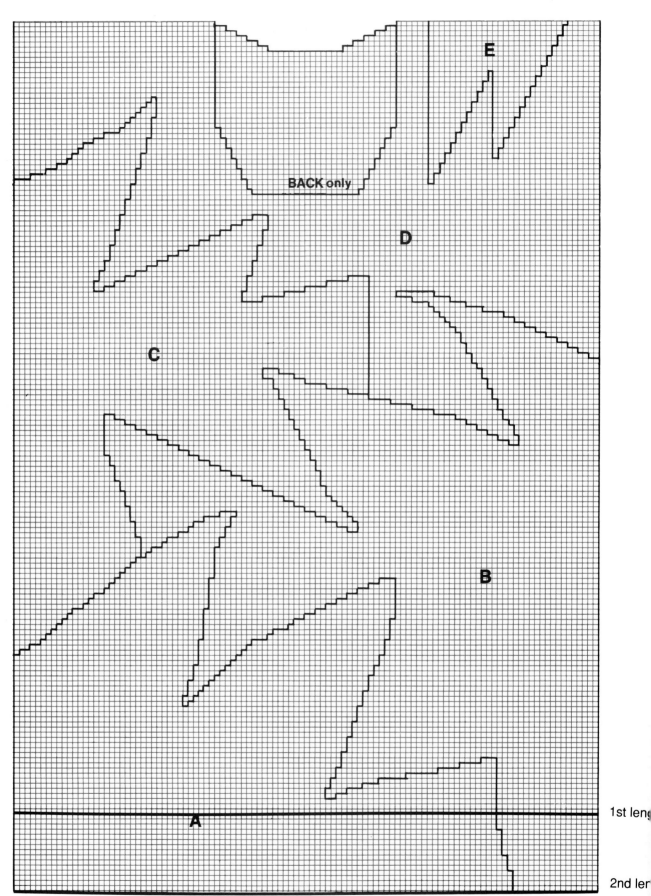

E

BACK only

D

C

B

A

1st leng

2nd ler

Add 15 rows for 3rd length

Hint for Intarsia

Use a separate ball every time a new colour appears.

When you join in each of the new colours tie a neat knot and leave 10 cm (4 ") tails. Weave these in each stitch at the back while that colour lasts on the graph then leave them till the next row if necessary. If the width of the new colour is too narrow to use this method leave the tail and sew it in later along the edge of the colour change.

There is no armhole shaping for a drop shoulder style. Shape the back neck hole as indicated.

Cast off (bind off) straight across the last row loosely so the shoulders will stretch comfortably. Work one stitch ahead for a neat finish.

Front

As for the back but this time shape the hole for the neck as indicated on the graph. Divide the two shoulders by putting the 20 central stitches on a stitch holder or a safety pin. This will make it easier to pick up for the neckband and will help make the neck elastic. Decrease one each side every row for 10 rows. Continue straight for the remaining rows. Cast off loosely.

Sleeve

The sleeves are exactly the same as each other. Do not make them a mirror image.

Cast on loosely 40 stitches using the band needles. Rib as for the bottom band. Then increase on a purl row evenly to 60 stitches using the body needles.

Continue in stocking stitch (stockinette) using the central 60 sts of the front graph and then increasing one stitch each edge every 4th row. To match the increases for sewing the sleeve seam knit into the front and then the back of the first stitch. Complete the row till two stitches remain. Knit into the front and then the back of the next stitch, knit the last stitch.

When the sleeve is long enough cast off very loosely regardless of the graph. The average sleeve is 50 cms in length.

Neck Band

Sew one shoulder seam using the Weaving method. Use straight needles and make a seam or sew both shoulder use round needles or four needles.

Using a "band" needle like a crochet hook and the yarn which matches the top of the garment, face the front of the work and knit up stitches evenly around the

hole as follows: 30 from the back of the neck, 18 along the straight vertical edge, 13 along the diagonal, knit the 20 from the safety pin to carry the yarn with you, then 13 and then 18. (Total=112 stitches)

To avoid holes in the corners ignore that space and pick up stitches from either side of it.

Rib as for the band.

Cast off (bind off) very loosely in rib.

Sew the remaining shoulder seam. Sew the band seam using the Up through the Bar method.

Fold neckband inside and sew down each stitch.

To Make Up

This should be done from the outside using two different techniques: Weaving and Up through the Bar.

Sew the sleeve seams including the ribbed bands using the Up through the Bar method. Reinforce the beginning of the cuff.

Lay the garment flat and find the armpit by stretching the cast off (bind off) row of the sleeve as deep as possible (at least 28 cm or 11 inches from the shoulder seam.) Tie the front to the back at this point on both sides of the body.

Side seams

Use the Up through the Bar method for both the ribbed bands and the stocking stitch (stockinette) side seams. Begin at the band and reinforce the first few stitches. Sew up to the ties at the arm pits. Reinforce again.

Setting in the sleeves

Alternate every stitch using the Weaving method for the sleeve stitches and the Up through the Bar method for the body rows.

Five stitches from the sleeve will match seven rows from the body as for any drop shoulder garment.

Check the inside for any remaining tails and sew these in along the edges of the colour change using a large eyed needle.

Alternative Colourways

The original is navy, petral, spruce, grey and lilac and also shown in nut brown, brick, gold, and cream. Alternatives are:
Black, navy, princess blue, saxe blue and gray

Black, princess blue, saxe blue, red and white
Black, princess blue, red, gold and black again

Key Design Elements

The changes in direction between one block of colour and the next, and the grading of the colours, are the keys.

Paw Prints

Black paw prints mark the warm, random background. Some black from the paw prints peeking through the background colour is an asset not a problem. (The puppies have hairy paws!)

The background is constantly changing using a range of warm neutrals working from the darkest at the bottom up to the lightest at the top. The paw print graph of 20 sts and 20 rows is followed by 20 rows without fairisle; just the colour changes of your choice. The yarns can be cut and tied at any point including in the middle of a row.

The subtly of the colour changes are in your hands. Don't try to repeat them on the back and sleeves. Just play and enjoy. You can always go back later and swiss darn or duplicate stitch partial rows in another colour.

Yarns Required
UNIQUE 8 ply
   black 407 x 7
UNIQUE 8 ply
   gold 404 x 1
UNIQUE 8 ply
   natural cream 423 x 1
UNIQUE 8 ply
   brick red 406 x 1
UNIQUE 8 ply
   brown 405 x 2
UNIQUE 8 ply
   camel 401 x 2
UNIQUE 8 ply
   mushroom 400 x 2
UNIQUE 8 ply
   pale pink 414 x 1
UNIQUE 8 ply
   apricot 416 x 1
ANGORA SUPREME
   camel 1361 x 1

Plus a total of 100 gms of mixed yarns including five different types of creamy textured yarns.

Needles
3.5 mm (U.S.#4, U.K.#9)
   needles for the bottom
   bands, cuffs and
   neckband
4.5 mm (U.S.#6, U.K .#7)
   needles for the body

Tension or Gauge
stocking stitch (stockinette)
21 sts and 25 rows
to 10 cm (4 inches) over the
paw prints (fairisle.)

21 sts and 27 rows
to 10 cm (4 inches) over the
stocking stitch (stockinette)

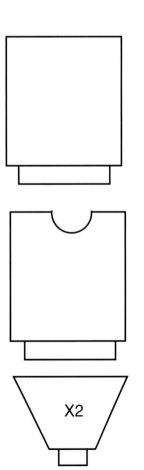

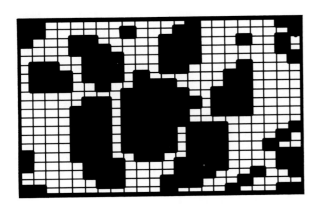

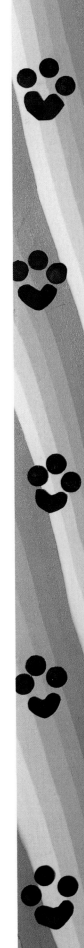

Our model is wearing the middle size for width and the first size for length.

Back

Cast on loosely 100 (120, 140) sts using the band needles. Work the band in rib for 27 rows. Work the first four rows in black and then the next 19 in a range of different yarns (dark) and the last four in black again.

Change to the body needles and do a purl row increasing to 110 (132, 154) sts evenly across the row.

Carry the black and one other yarn of your choice across the row. Change the background colour every two or three rows. If you like a soft rolling look then change to a closely related colour.

Read the graph beginning from the bottom right corner and read left for the first row and right for the second. You may find it easier to tip the graph upside down to read every second row if you are not very experienced.

Repeat the graph 5 (6, 7) times across the row.

Hint for Fairisle

Carry the yarn very loosely across the back. Tension that looks loose enough at the time of knitting will pucker after a few more rows have been worked. To avoid this common problem work with your stitches

Garment Size

Body Width: 50 cm or 19^1/$_2$", (60 cm or 23^1/$_2$", 70 cm or 27^1/$_2$")

Stitch numbers = 110 (132, 154) or any additional 22 sts.

Total Length: 60 cm or 23^1/$_2$", (65 cm or 25^1/$_2$", 70 cm or 27^1/$_2$")

Row numbers = 156, (169, 182)

Any combination can be made depending on your needs.

central 20 sts on a holder. Add a background yarn to the side without yarn and work both sides at once. Decrease one each neck edge, each front facing row for a total of 10 rows. (This makes five decreases each side.) Continue straight for 20 rows. Cast off (bind off) straight across the last row loosely so the shoulders will stretch comfortably.

Sleeve

Cast on loosely 40 stitches using the band needles. Rib as the bottom band for 27 rows. Increase on a purl row evenly to 66 stitches using the body needles. Work three graph patterns across the row and continue as for body increasing one stitch each edge every 4th row. To match the increases for sewing the sleeve seam knit into the front and then the back of the first stitch. Complete the row till two stitches remain. Knit into the front and then the back of the next stitch, knit the last stitch.

Work the deeper colours up further on the sleeve because the drop shoulder will bring the light colours at the top of the body over into the top of the sleeve.

When the sleeve is long enough cast off very loosely.

Neck Band

Sew one shoulder seam using the Weaving method. Use straight needles and make a seam or sew both

spread out on your needles and carry very loosely at the back.

After working the 20 rows of the fairisle graph change to normal stocking stitch for 20 rows. The width of your knitting should not change. This is a good check on your fairisle technique.

Continue working 20 rows of fairisle and 20 rows of stocking stitch (stockinette), getting lighter and lighter as you work towards the chest and shoulders.

Change colour in the middle of a row and as often as you wish. To

encourage the random element, cut and tie short lengths of yarn in the general colour range in advance. As you are knitting, cut and add in a different colour as required.

There is no armhole shaping for a drop shoulder and no neck shaping on the back of this garment. Work until the back is long enough then cast off loosely.

Front

As back until neck shaping. Shape the neck as follows:

Work until the front is 30 rows shorter than the back (12 cm or 5 inches.) Put the shoulders and use round needles or four needles.

Using a "band" needle like a crochet hook and black or the yarn which matches the top of the garment, face the front of the work and knit up stitches evenly around the hole as follows:

30 from the back of the neck, 17 along the straight vertical edge, 8 along the diagonal, knit the 20 from the safety pin to carry the yarn with you, then 8 and then 17. (Total 100 sts.) To avoid holes in the corners ignore that space and pick up stitches from either side of it.

Work the band pattern for 27 rows adding the black bands as desired. Cast off (bind off) very loosely in rib.

Sew the remaining shoulder seam. Sew the neck band seam using the Up through the Bar method.

Fold the neckband inside and sew each stitch to its matching picked up stitch loosely to allow for stretch.

To Make Up
This should be done from the outside using two different techniques: Weaving and Up through the Bar.

Sew the sleeve seams including the ribbed bands using the Up through the Bar method. Reinforce the

beginning of the cuff.

Lay the garment flat and find the armpit by stretching the cast off (bind off) row of the sleeve as deep as possible (at least 28 cm or 11") from the shoulder seam. Tie the front to the back at this point on both sides of the body.

Side seams
Use the Up through the Bar method for both the ribbed bands and the stocking stitch (stockinette) side seams. Begin at the band and reinforce the first few stitches. Sew up to the ties at the arm pits.

Reinforce again.

Setting in the sleeves
Alternate every stitch using the Weaving method for the sleeve stitches and the Up through the Bar method for the body rows.

Five stitches from the sleeve will match seven rows from the body as for any drop shoulder garment.

Check the inside for any remaining tails and sew these in along the edges of the colour change using a large eyed needle.

Alternative Colourways
The background colours in the original garment are soft including pink and apricot but the black paw prints add a stark contrast for strength.

If you wish to change the colours of this design keep the top in the brighter or lighter colours and the bottom in the darker or cooler colours. The graded colour accentuates the male physique.

Any group of colours will work if they start dark at the bottom and work up to lighter over the shoulders. Think in terms of a double-barrelled colour like blue-green or blue-grey or gold-pink or red-brown or grey-brown or plum-purple. This will suggest the range of colours to you. Choose at least 10 yarns to play with that will cover the range. Some angora or mohair will give a soft, fluffy look.

Key Design Element
The light shoulders and dark hips are the key. Any repeat pattern in black will work over this background.

How I Love Thee

The bright abstracted letters spell the title but these are not obvious to the uninitiated. Read from the top left shoulder down to the point of the vee and back up again. The hearts are more obvious. This design is a good sharing sweater. First up = best dressed. Alternatively, make a matching set and change the colours. Different colourways are given at the end.

Yarns Required

A: UNIQUE 8 ply
   red 414 x 6
B: UNIQUE 8 ply
   saxe blue 421 x 4
C: UNIQUE 8 ply
   gold 404 x 2
D: UNIQUE 8 ply
   black 407 x 2
E: UNIQUE 8 ply
   princess blue 410 x 1
F: UNIQUE 8ply
   purple 408 x 1
G: UNIQUE 8 ply
   white 403 x 1
H: ANGORA SUPREME
   hot pink 1358 x $^1/2$

Needles

3.5 mm (U.S.#4 U.K.#10)
   needles for the bands,
   cuff and neckband.
4 mm (U.S.#6, U.K.#8)
   needles for the body.

Tension or Gauge

stocking stitch (stockinette)
22 sts and 30 rows
to 10 cm (4 inches)

Garment Size

Body Width: 50 cm or
   19 $^1/2$" (60 cm or 23$^1/2$",
   70 cm or 27$^1/2$")
Stitch numbers = 110 (132,
   154)
Total Length: 60 cm or
   23$^1/2$" (65 cm or 25$^1/2$",
   70 cm or 27$^1/2$")
Row numbers = 180 (195,
   210)

The graph shows the smallest size.

To increase the width

Halve the extra stitches that you need and add them onto either side of the graph. Work the extra stitches in the main background colour on that side.

Back

Cast on loosely 100 (120, 140) sts using the band needles. Work the band in rib for 25 rows.

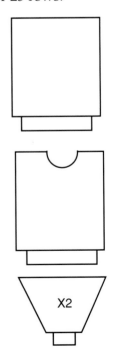

45

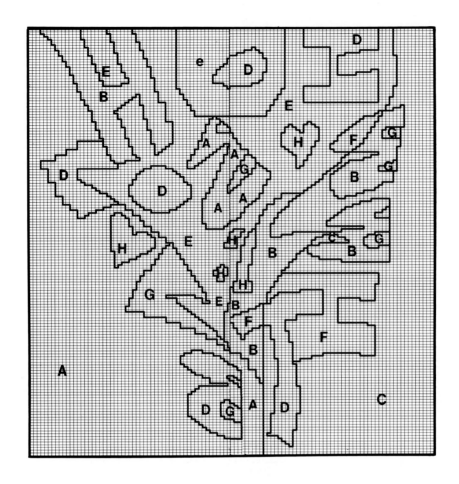

Change to the body needles and do a purl row increasing to 110 (132, 154) sts evenly across the row.

You are now ready to begin the graph in stocking stitch (stockinette.)

Read the graph beginning from the bottom right corner and read left for the first row and right for the second. You may find it easier to tip the graph upside down to read every second row if you are not very experienced.

Use a separate ball every time a new colour appears.

Hint for Intarsia

When you join in each of the new colours tie a neat knot and leave 10 cm (4") tails. Weave these in each stitch at the back while that colour lasts on the graph then leave them till the next row if necessary. If the width of the new colour is too narrow to use this method leave the tail and sew it in later along the edge of the colour change.

There is no armhole shaping for a drop shoulder style and no neck shaping on the back so continue the graph filling in the hole for the front neck shaping with matching colours.

Cast off (bind off) straight across the last row loosely so the shoulders will stretch comfortably.

Front

As for the back, but this time shape the hole for the neck as indicated on the graph. Divide the two shoulders by putting the 20 central stitches on a stitch holder or a safety pin. This will make it easier to pick up for the neckband and will also help make the neck more elastic. Decrease one each side every row for 10 rows.

47

Continue straight for the remaining rows until the front matches the back in length. Cast off loosely.

Sleeve

The sleeves are exactly the same as each other. Do not make them a mirror image.

Cast on loosely 40 stitches using the band needles. Rib as for the bottom band. Then increase on a purl row evenly to 50 stitches using the body needles.

Continue in stocking stitch (stockinette) using the central 50 sts of the graph and increasing one stitch each edge every 4th row. To match the increases for sewing the sleeve seam knit into the front and then the back of the first stitch. Complete the row till two stitches remain. Knit into the front and then the back of the next stitch, knit the last stitch.

When the sleeve is long enough cast off very loosely. The average sleeve is 50 cm in length.

Neck Band

Sew one shoulder seam using the Weaving method. Use straight needles and make a seam or sew both shoulders and use round needles or four needles.

Using a "band" needle like a crochet hook and the band yarn or the yarn which matches the top of the garment, face the front of the work and knit up stitches evenly around the hole as follows:

30 from the back of the neck, 18 along the straight vertical edge, 13 along the diagonal, knit the 20 from the safety pin to carry the yarn with you, then 13 and then 18. (Total=112 stitches) To avoid holes in the corners ignore that space and pick up stitches from either side of it.

Rib as for the band. Cast off (bind off) very loosely in rib.

Sew the remaining shoulder seam. Sew the band seam using the Up through the Bar method. Fold shoulder seam inwards. Sew each stitch loosely.

To Make Up

This should be done from the outside using two different techniques: Weaving and Up through the Bar.

Sew the sleeve seams including the ribbed bands using the Up through the Bar method. Reinforce the beginning of the cuff.

Lay the garment flat and find the armpit by stretching the cast off (bind off) row of the sleeve as deep as possible (at least 28 cms or 11 inches from the shoulder seam.) Tie the front to the back at this point on both sides of the body to mark the armpit.

Side seams

Use the Up through the Bar method for both the ribbed bands and the stocking stitch (stockinette) side seams. Begin at the band and reinforce the first few stitches. Sew up to the ties at the arm pits. Reinforce again.

Setting in the sleeves

Alternate every stitch using the Weaving method for the sleeve stitches and the Up through the Bar method for the body rows.

Five stitches from the sleeve will match seven rows from the body as for any drop shoulder garment.

Check the inside for any remaining tails and sew these in along the edges of the colour change using a large eyed needle.

Alternative Colourways

Any bright colours will work. Just have fun. For a low key look, work in black and white and grey. The letters can be differentiated by shades of grey or by textured yarns in a range of fibres or by stitch types. Add hot pink or pale pink hearts.

Change the heart colour to blue if your love is unrequited or to green if you are a nature lover.

Key Design Elements

The letters form a vee shape which draws the eye up and out over the shoulders.

49

Cubist Kiss

Painters throughout history have used the human face as the basis for experimentation.

Yarns Required

A: UNIQUE 8 ply
   black 407 x 5

B: UNIQUE 8 ply
   navy 409 x 2

C: UNIQUE 8 ply
   bottle 422 x 2

D: UNIQUE 8 ply
   purple 408 x 1

E: UNIQUE 8 ply
   red 414 x 1

F: UNIQUE 8 ply
   melon 412 x 2

G: UNIQUE 8 ply
   gold 404 x 1

H: UNIQUE 8 ply
   saxe blue 421 x 3

I: UNIQUE 8 ply
   princess blue 410 x 3

J: ANGORA SUPREME
   hot pink 1358 x 1

K: ANGORA SUPREME
   white 1351 x 1

L: Pink mohair x $^1/_2$

Needles

3.5 mm (U.S.#4, U.K.#10)
   needles for the bands,
   cuff and neckband.

4 mm (U.S.#6, U.K.#8)
   needles for the body.

Tension or Gauge

stocking stitch (stockinette)
22 sts and 30 rows
to 10 cm (4 inches)

Garment Size

Body Width: 55cms or
   21$^1/_2$" (60 cm or 23$^1/_2$",
   70 cms or 27$^1/_2$")

Stitch numbers = 120 (132,
   154)

Total Length: 60 cms or
   23 $^1/_2$" (65 cms or 25$^1/_2$",
   70 cms or 27$^1/_2$")

Row numbers = 180 (195,
   210)

The model is wearing the
first size in both width and
length but any
combinations may be made
depending on your needs.
The additional sizes in
brackets indicate the extra
stitches and rows for larger
sizes.

To increase the width
Halve the extra stitches that
you need and add them
onto either side of the
graph. Work the extra
stitches in the main
background colour on that
side.

More experienced knitters
may wish to extend the
design lines and work with
all of the colours indicated
on the outside edges.

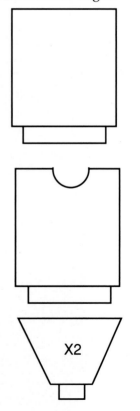

X2

51

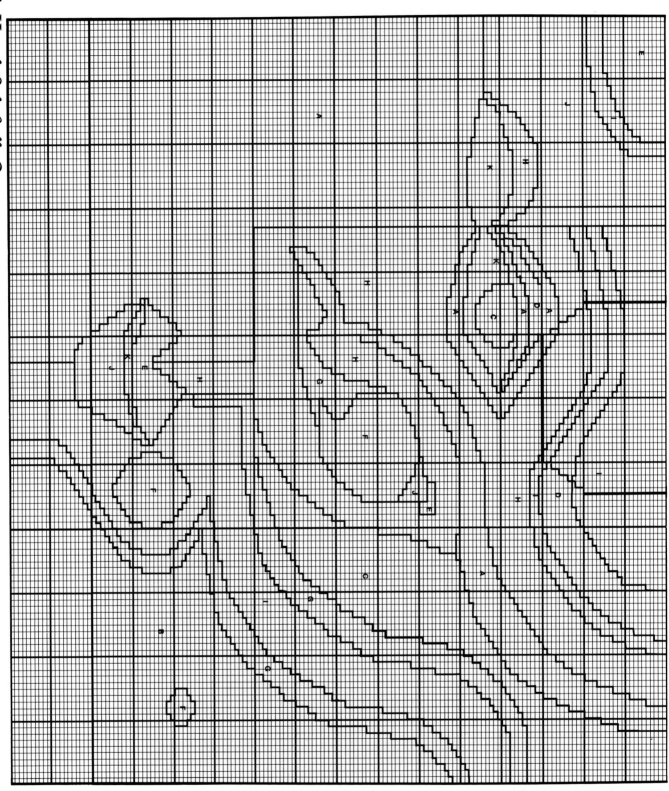

To increase the length

Increase before beginning the graph if the additional length is preplanned or continue the graph delaying the neck shaping.

Back

Cast on loosely 110 (120, 140) sts using the band needles. Work the band in rib for 25 rows.

Change to the body needles and do a purl row increasing to 120 (132,154) sts evenly across the row.

You are now ready to begin the graph in stocking stitch (stockinette.)

Read the graph beginning from the bottom right corner and read left for the first row and right for the second. You may find it easier to tip the graph upside down to read every second row if you are not very experienced.

Use a separate ball every time a new colour appears.

Hint for Intarsia

When you join in each of the new colours tie a neat knot and leave 10 cm (4 ") tails. Weave these in each stitch at the back while that colour lasts on the graph then leave them till the next row if necessary.

If the width of the new colour is too narrow to use this method leave the tail and sew it in later along the edge of the colour change.

There is no armhole shaping for a drop shoulder style and no neck shaping on the back so continue the graph filling in the hole for the front neck shaping.

Cast off (bind off) straight across the last row loosely so the shoulders will stretch comfortably.

Front

As for the back but this time shape the hole for the neck as indicated on the graph. Divide the two shoulders by putting the 20 central stitches on a stitch holder or a safety pin. This will make it easier to pick up for the neckband and will help make the neck elastic. Decrease one each side every row for 10 rows.

Continue straight for the remaining rows. Cast off loosely.

Sleeve

The sleeves are exactly the same as each other. Do not make them a mirror image.

Cast on loosely 40 stitches using the band needles. Rib as for the bottom band. Then increase on a purl row evenly to 60 stitches using the body needles.

Continue in stocking stitch (stockinette) using the graph and increasing one stitch each edge every 4th row. To match the increases for sewing the sleeve seam knit into the front and then the back of the first stitch.

Complete the row till two stitches remain. Knit into the front and then the back of the next stitch, knit the last stitch.

When the sleeve is long enough cast off very loosely. The average sleeve is 50 cms in length.

Neck Band

Sew one shoulder seam using the Weaving method. Use straight needles and make a seam or sew both shoulders and use round needles or four needles.

Using a "band" needle like a crochet hook and the band yarn or the yarn which matches the top of the garment, face the front of the work and knit up stitches evenly around the hole as follows:

30 from the back of the neck, 18 along the straight vertical edge, 13 along the diagonal, knit the 20 from the safety pin to carry the yarn with you, then 13 and then 18. (Total=112 stitches)

To avoid holes in the corners ignore that space and pick up stitches from either side of it.

Rib as for the band. Cast off (bind off) very loosely in rib.

Sew the remaining shoulder seam.

Sew the neck band seam using the Up through the

53

Five stitches from the sleeve will match seven rows from the body as for any drop shoulder garment.

Check the inside for any remaining tails and sew these in along the edges of the colour change using a large eyed needle.

Alternative Colourways
The original is in bright colours with a blue background. Change to all neutrals or to warm autumn colours or work the whole design in black and white and a range of greys. (A) should be black and (B) the darkest grey.

If working with black and white and grey keep the outsides of the eyes (K) in white. The irises in a bright blue or green in an otherwise black and white sweater will draw the attention.

For a more feminine version work in mohair and embroider sweeping eyelashes on the eyes. Add metallics into the eyeshadow area and use silk or rayon for the lips to add a gloss.

Key Design Elements
The eyes and the lips! Eyes are such a powerful image it is easier to wear them when they are abstracted rather than realistic. A person holding a conversation with you may become distracted and talk to the sweater instead.

Bar method. Fold inwards and sew down each stitch allowing for stretch.

To Make Up
This should be done from the outside using two different techniques: Weaving and Up through the Bar.

Sew the sleeve seams including the ribbed bands using the Up through the Bar method. Reinforce the beginning of the cuff.

Lay the garment flat and find the armpit by stretching the cast off (bind off) row of the sleeve as deep as possible (at least 28 cm or 11 inches from the shoulder seam.) Tie the front to the back at this point on both sides of the body.

Side seams
Use the Up through the Bar method for both the ribbed bands and the stocking stitch (stockinette) side seams. Begin at the band and reinforce the first few stitches. Sew up to the ties at the arm pits.

Reinforce again.

Setting in the sleeves
Alternate every stitch using the Weaving method for the sleeve stitches and the Up through the Bar method for the body rows.

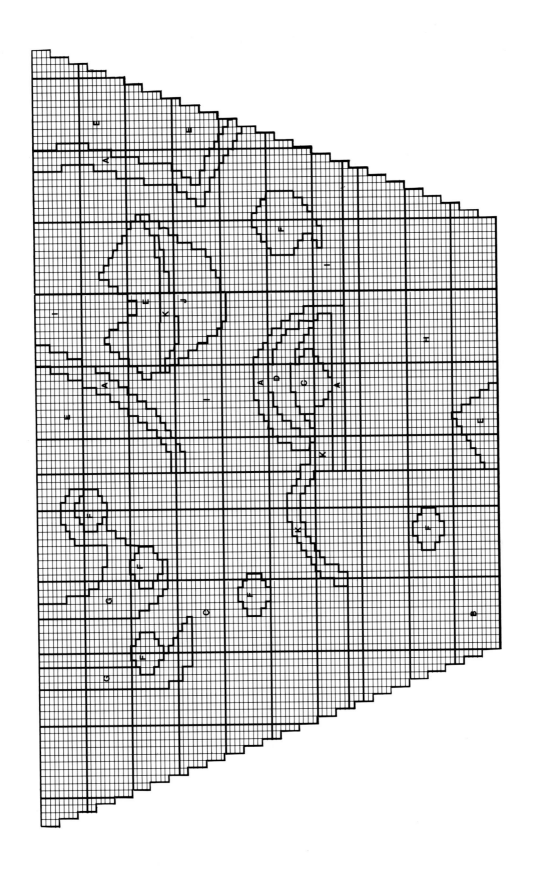

55

Gold Rock

This design encompasses both the richness of the sound of jazz and the wealth of gold buried beneath the earth in seams and nuggets. They are exposed here for anyone with a heart of gold. The scribbles of "jazz energy" are embroidered later, in stem stitch.

Yarns Required

A: UNIQUE 12 ply
    black 507 x 6

B: CHANSON
    claret 948 x 4

C: UNIQUE 12 ply
    gold 504 x 1

D: UNIQUE 12 ply
    purple 508 x 2

E: UNIQUE 12 ply
    red x 1

F: Cleckheaton COLLAGE
    red 1208 x 2

G: Cleckheaton COLLAGE
    taupe and red 1209 x 2

H: Cleckheaton
    SENSATION
    red 1275 x 4

I: Metallic Bronze 12 ply x 1

Needles

5 mm (U.S.#7, U.K.#6)
    needles for the bands,
    cuff and neckband.

6 mm (U.S.#9, U.K.#4)
    needles for the body.

Tension or Gauge

stocking stitch (stockinette)
16 sts and 21 rows
to l0cm (4 inches)

Garment size

Width: 56 cm or 22" (62 cm
    or 24^1/$_2$", 74 cm or 29")

Total stitches = 90 (100, 120)

Length: 60 cm or 23^1/$_2$",
    (65 cm or 25^1/$_2$", 70 cm or
    27^1/$_2$")

Total rows = 132 (142,152)
The graph is the middle
width and full length.

Back

Cast on loosely 80 sts (90,
100) sts using the band
needles in (A). Work the
band for a total of 25 rows
in rib. To do "Rib" knit 1,
purl l, across the row. If you
end with a knit stitch begin
the next row with a purl.

Change to the body needles
and do a purl row
increasing to 90 (100, 120)

sts evenly across the row.
Begin the graph.

Reading a Graph

One stitch is represented by
one square. Read from the
bottom right hand corner to

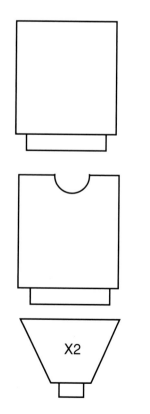

57

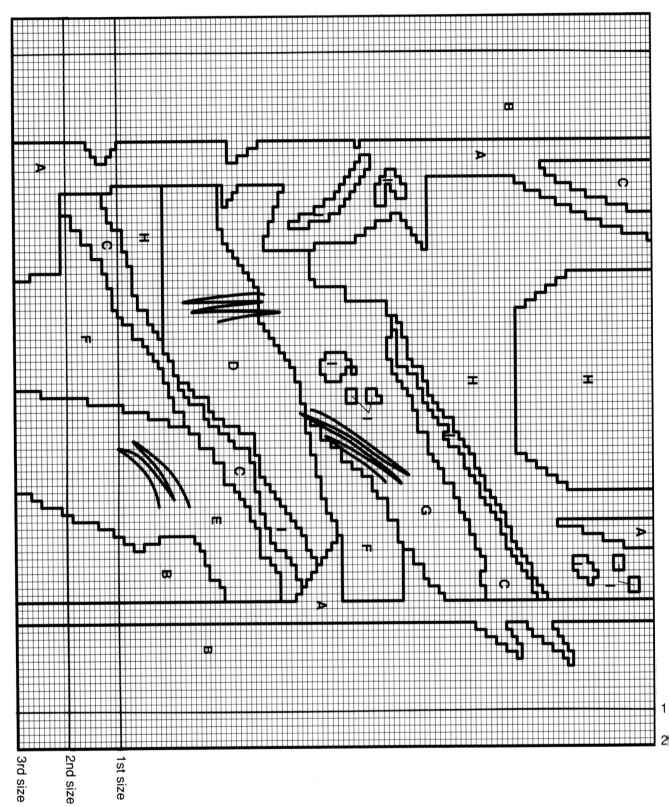

3rd size
2nd size
1st size

Add 10 to each side for largest size.

sew it in later along the edge of the colour change.

Completing the back

There is no armhole shaping for a drop shoulder style and no neck shaping on the back. Fill in the neck hole on the back continuing in the basic design idea already established.

Cast off (bind off) straight across the last row maintaining the colours.

Front

As for the back but this time shape the hole for the neck as shown on the graph.

26 rows from the end divide the two shoulders by putting the 20 central stitches on a stitch holder or a safety pin. This will make it easier to pick up for the neckband and will help make the neck elastic. Decrease one stitch every 2nd row for 10 rows (five decreases in all). Continue straight for 16 rows. Cast off maintaining the colours.

Sleeve

Both sleeves are the same. Do not mirror image them. Cast on 35 stitches using the band needles. Work the band as for the bottom back band. Change to the body needles. Increase on a purl row evenly to 50 stitches using the body needles.

Use the central 50 stitches of the front graph but also increase one stitch each edge every 4th row.

the left for the first knit row. Take special care for the first row because it establishes the position of all stitches above it.

Read from left to right for the purl row even though you will still be knitting from right to left. Turn the graph upside down if it helps.

Hint for Intarsia

When you join in each of the new colours tie a neat knot and leave 10 cm (4 ") tails. Weave these in behind each stitch at the back while that colour lasts on the graph then leave them till the next row if necessary. If the width of the new colour is too narrow to use this method leave the tail and

Continue increasing every 4th row until the sleeve is long enough. Change the colours on the second sleeve if you wish but do not mirror image it.

When the sleeve is long enough cast off very loosely. The average sleeve will end after the 95th row of the graph.

Neck Band

Sew one shoulder seam using the Weaving method and using the matching colours. Use straight needles and make a seam or sew both shoulders and use round needles or four needles. Use a "band" needle like a crochet hook, and (H) or whichever coloured yarn you feel works best by the face. Facing the front of the work, knit up stitches evenly around the hole as follows: 30 from the back of the neck, 13 along the straight vertical edge, 7 along the diagonal, knit the 20 from the safety pin to carry the yarn with you, then 7 and then 13. (Total= 90 stitches)

To avoid holes in the corners ignore that space and pick up stitches from either side of it. Rib for 25 rows.

Cast off (bind off) very loosely in rib using a "body" needle if necessary. Sew the band seam using the Up through the Bar method and the remaining shoulder seam using the Weaving method. Fold the neckband inside. Sew each stitch down to its matching "picked up" stitch but make the loops slightly loose to allow the neck to stretch.

Sewing Up

This should be done from the outside using two different techniques: Weaving and Up through the Bar.

Sew the sleeve seams including the ribbed bands using the Up through the Bar method. Reinforce the beginning of the cuff as this will be under a lot of stress over the years.

Side seams

Use the Up through the Bar method for both the ribbed bands and the stocking stitch (stockinette) side seams. Begin at the band and reinforce the first few stitches. Sew side seams to within 28 cm (11") of the shoulder seam. Reinforce again.

Setting in the sleeves

Alternate every stitch using the Weaving method for the sleeve stitches and the Up through the Bar method for the body rows.

Five stitches from the sleeve will match seven rows from the body as for any drop shoulder garment.

Check the inside for any remaining tails and sew these in along the edges of the colour change using a large eyed needle.

Embroidery

Work the black scribbles in stem stitch. They are important to balance the strength of the colours.

Alternative colourways

The original is in reds and gold and black with bronze metallic thread.

Larger areas of gold or more metallics yarns would work well. Any of the yarns can be substituted, but maintain the weight to avoid distortion.

Use metallic effects up by the face and shoulder area to make the most effective use of the yarns.

When working with fine metallics in a large area of the sweater, twist them with a strong wool to add elasticity. Avoid using them in the cuffs and bottom bands.

With a title, Gold Rock, the colours should stay warm for this design but the graph will adapt to any colour range. Think about a sweater named Frozen Rock, or Lava Rock, or alternatively, Classic Rock or Light Rock.

Key Design Elements

The dark sides and diagonal divisions within the centre panel add height and slim the hips. The metallic effect is key to the title and the concept.

Outlet

Electrical wiring and plugs suggested this intarsia design. The waving cords end in a rectangular block complete with two prongs.

Yarns Required

A: UNIQUE 12 ply
purple 508 x 1

B: UNIQUE 12 ply
gold 504 x 2

C: UNIQUE 12 ply
nut brown 520 x 8

D: Cleckheaton COLLAGE
grey 1199 x 1

E: UNIQUE 8 ply
light brown 405 x 1 used
double

F: UNIQUE 12 ply
navy 509 x 5

G: textured yarn or (D)

H: Cleckheaton MOHAIR
12 ply
red orange 1466 x 1

I: UNIQUE 12 ply
black 507 x scrap

J: Cleckheaton SENSATION
black 1271 x 1

K: Cleckheaton
SENSATION
red 1275 x 1

M: UNIQUE 8 ply
bottle 422 x 1 used double

Needles

4.5 mm (U.S.#6, U.K.#7)
needles for the bands,
cuff and neckband.

6 mm (U.S.#9, U.K.#4)
needles for the body.

Tension or Gauge

stocking stitch (stockinette)
17 sts and 22 rows
to l0 cm (4 inches)

Garment Size

Width: 53 cm or 21" (58 cm
or 23", 70 cm or 27^1/$_2$")

Total stitches = 90 (100, 120)

Length: 60 cm or 23^1/$_2$",
(65 cm or 25^1/$_2$")

Total rows = 132 (142)

Back Band

Cast on loosely 80 (90, 100)
sts using the band needles
in (C). Work the band for a
total of 25 rows in ribbing.

Change to the body needles
and do a purl row
increasing to 90 (100, 120)
sts evenly across the row.
Begin the graph. Add 5 sts
to each side for first size, 10
for the second size and 20
for the third size.

Reading a Graph

One stitch is represented by
one square. Read from the
bottom right hand corner to
the left for the first knit row.
Take special care for the
first row because it
establishes the position of
all stitches above it.

Turn the graph upside
down to read the purl rows.

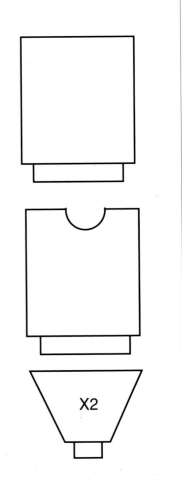

X2

63

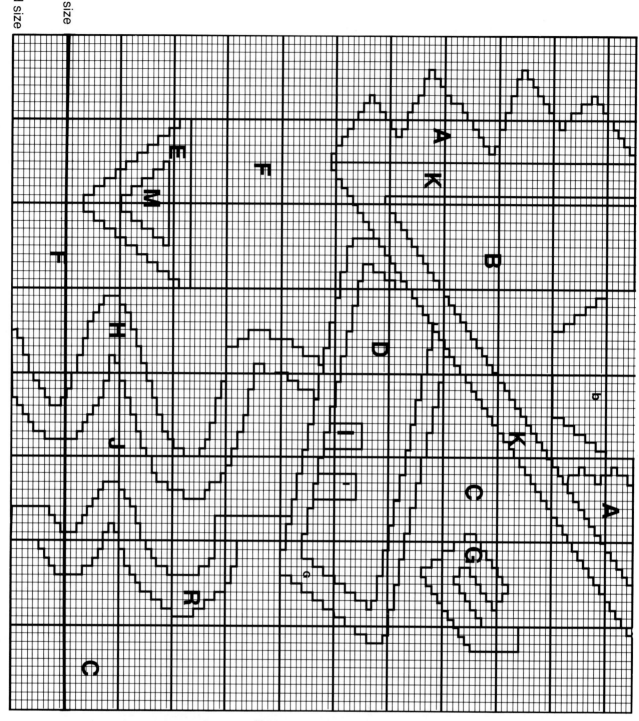

Completing the back

There is no armhole shaping for a drop shoulder style and no neck shaping on the back. Fill in the neck hole on the back continuing in the basic design idea already established.

Cast off (bind off) straight across the last row maintaining the colours.

Front

As for the back but this time shape the hole for the neck as shown on the graph.

16 rows from the end divide the two shoulders by putting the 10 central stitches on a stitch holder or a safety pin. This will make it easier to pick up for the neckband and will help

make the neck elastic. Decrease one stitch every 2nd row for 10 rows (five decreases in all). Continue straight for 6 rows. Cast off maintaining the colours.

Sleeve

Both sleeves are the same. Do not mirror image them. Cast on 35 stitches using the band needles. Work the

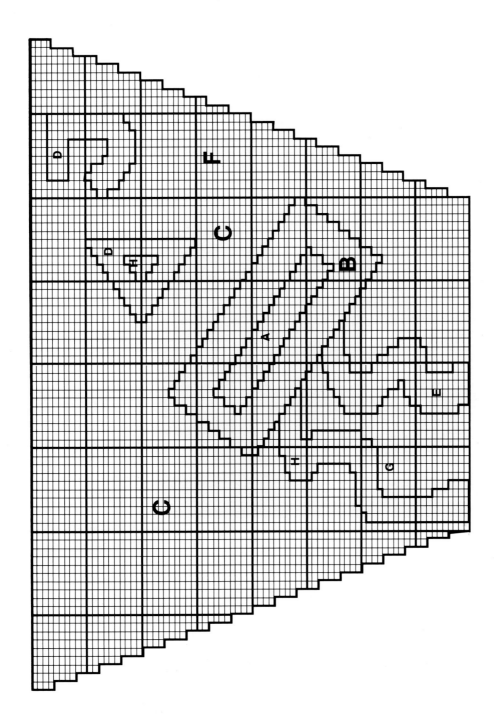

band as for the bottom back band. Change to the body needles. Increase on a purl row evenly to 50 stitches using the body needles.

Continue increasing every 4th row until the sleeve is long enough. Change the colours on the second sleeve if you wish but do not mirror image it.

When the sleeve is long enough cast off very loosely. The average sleeve will end after the 95th row of the graph.

Neck Band
Sew one shoulder seam using the Weaving method and using the matching colours. Use straight needles and make a seam or

sew both shoulders and use round needles or four needles. Using a "band" needle like a crochet hook, (B) coloured yarn and facing the front of the work knit up stitches evenly around the hole as follows:

20 from the back of the neck, 8 along the straight vertical edge, 10 along the

seams. Begin at the band and reinforce the first few stitches. Sew side seams to within 28cm (11") of shoulder seam. Reinforce again.

Setting in the sleeves
Alternate every stitch using the Weaving method for the sleeve stitches and the Up through the Bar method for the body rows.

Five stitches from the sleeve will match seven rows from the body as for any drop shoulder garment.

Check the inside for any remaining tails and sew these in along the edges of the colour change using a large eyed needle.

Alternative Colourways
Any colours will work if they are all intense.

The original is in warm gold and brown.

Alternatives are:
navy with red and gold,
black with bright blue and green,
purple with bottle green and red.

Key Design Elements
The oversize graphic is strongly coloured and full of diagonals and waves which generate a feeling of movement. Parts of the bold design repeat on the sleeves in a different form or in different colours.

diagonal, knit the 10 from the safety pin to carry the yarn with you, then 10 and then 8. (Total = 66 stitches)

To avoid holes in the corners ignore that space and pick up stitches from either side of it. Rib for 25 rows. Cast off (bind off) very loosely in rib using a "body" needle if necessary.

Sew the band seam using the Up through the Bar method and the remaining shoulder seam using the Weaving method. Fold the neckband inside. Sew each stitch down to its matching "picked up" stitch but make the loops slightly loose to allow the neck to stretch.

Sewing Up
This should be done from the outside using two different techniques: Weaving and Up through the Bar.

Sew the sleeve seams including the ribbed bands using the Up through the Bar method. Reinforce the beginning of the cuff.

Side seams
Use the Up through the Bar method for both the ribbed bands and the stocking stitch (stockinette) side

Side Bar

To create fabric, which appeals to both the hand and the eye, is an ideal. To create this fabric during the process of "play" is extra rewarding. This sweater is knitted sideways and the black bars are knitted in with the current colour.

Yarns Required
for Camel version on male
UNIQUE 12 ply
  black 507 x 5
UNIQUE 8 ply
  camel 401 x 3
UNIQUE 8 ply
  nut brown 420 x 4
UNIQUE 8 ply
  purple 408 x 1
UNIQUE 8 ply
  olive 415 x $^{1}/2$
UNIQUE 8 ply
  navy 409 x 1
Any extra textured yarns including lumpy light taupe cottons x 2

Yarns Required
for female
UNIQUE 12 ply
  black 507 x 4
UNIQUE 8 ply
  purple 408 x 4
UNIQUE 8 ply
  olive 415 x 1
UNIQUE 8 ply
  brick red 406 x 2
UNIQUE 8 ply
  navy 409 x 2
UNIQUE 8 ply
  petral 411 x 2

Cleckheaton NATURAL
  red 1275 x 1
Cleckheaton HIGHLAND
  8 ply brick 1130 x 1
Cleckheaton HIGHLAND
  8 ply lilac 1148 x 1
Cleckheaton SENSATION
  red 1275 x 1
Any extra textured yarns or mercerised cottons in:
slate blue, charcoal or hot pink x 1 each

To achieve a slimming appearance, use less of the light colours on the outsides of the body and more in the centre. The eye will see the body as curving away faster. Always use a dark colour for the main colour. This will be practical as well as slimming and will also enhance the other beautiful yarns.

Needles
4 mm (U.S. #5, U.K. #8) for
  the bands and cuffs
5 mm (U.S. #8, U.K. #5) for
  the body

Tension or Gauge
in stocking stitch 24 rows
17 sts to 10 cm (4 inches)

Garment Size
Body Width: 65 cm or 25^1/2"
Total Length: 70 cm or
  27^1/2"
  Wrist to Wrist: 165 cm or
  65^1/2" from (biggest
  size)
Sleeve Length: 50 cm or 20
  inches to drop shoulder
  (biggest size)

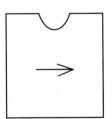

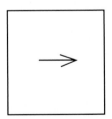

69

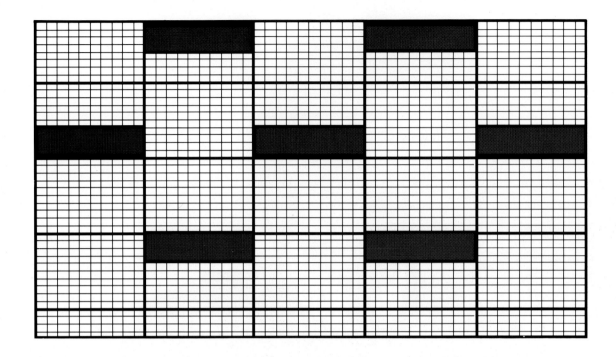

This garment is very adaptable to increasing the length and the width to absolutely any size even for an inexperienced knitter.

To increase the width
Halve the extra stitches that you need and add them to either side of the neckhole shaping on the front and add the total number to the back.

Add one stitch to the band for every two rows you have added to the body.

To alter the length
Alter the length by adding or subtracting stitches, not rows.

To decrease the width
Don't bother. It will work on a person with a 32" bust and hips. A little person will just need to make the sleeves shorter.

It is a good idea to divide up your yarn into 4 parts. This way the colours appear evenly through out the garment even if you only have a small amount.

Back
Cut some of the black UNIQUE 12 ply at the beginning into 115 cms or 45 inch lengths. These will be knitted along with your varying choices of 8 plys to make the raised bars.

Using any UNIQUE yarn cast on 100 sts loosely. Work in stocking stitch (stockinette) for 10 rows adding in new colours every row or two. Leave the yarn attached at the end and carry up the sides, cutting one every now and again, and introducing a new one.

Some of your more precious yarns will only be worked

in every 30 rows or so.

ROW 11: (front facing row)

Using both the black 12 ply and any 8 ply, knit together for the next 10 sts. Leave the black behind and continue using the 8 ply on its own. Add in a new strand of black 12 ply and knit the next 10 sts with both together. Leave the black behind. Continue in this fashion to the end of the row.

ROW 12: (back facing row)

Choose a new 8 ply and purl 10 sts then pick up the black and using both the 8 ply and the black 12 ply knit the next 10 sts. Purl the next 10 sts with just the 8 ply then pick up the black 12 ply and knit the next 10 sts. Continue in this fashion to the end of the row.

ROW 13: as row 11

ROW 14: as row 12

Do 10 more rows in stocking stitch (stockinette) in a range of 8 plys. Take the opportunity to weave in the tails of the black in the row immediately above.

ROW 25: *Knit 10 sts , 8 ply only. Using both 8 ply and black 12 ply, knit 10 sts. Repeat from *

ROW 26 to ROW 28: Repeat row 12 , 13 and 14 offsetting the black bars so they fall exactly in between those on row 11.

ROW 29 to ROW 39: Stocking stitch (stockinette.)

ROW 40: as row 11 Continue as above for a total of 144 rows without shaping. Cast off loosely.

Front

As for back but do not match the colour changes exactly. Continue until row 58. Shape neck as follows:

ROW 58: (front facing row) Cast off (bind off) 16 sts loosely.

Continue the row maintaining the pattern as established. (You may wish to ignore the black bars which will not be completed.)

For the next 10 rows decrease one st at the neck edge every row by working

2 sts together at the end and the beginning of the neck edge rows only.

At 74 sts, continue straight without neck shaping for 10 rows. This is an opportunity to correct your row count if necessary. Do more or less rows as necessary to begin the neck shaping at exactly the same point in the pattern as the decrease shaping ended.

Increase one st every row at the neck edge for 10 rows by working twice into the neck edge stitch.

Increase 16 sts by casting on loosely at the neck edge. (100 sts)

Continue straight for 58 rows in the established pattern. (Total 144 rows) Cast off (bind off) loosely.

Sleeve

Cast on 70 sts if you are tall and 60 if average and 50 if short, using 5 mm needles and any of the 8 plys.

Repeat the pattern from the back but change the colours.

Continue straight for at least 100 rows. Cast off loosely.

The second sleeve should have the colours in a different order.

Bottom band

Facing the front of the work and using black 12 ply UNIQUE and one 4 mm needle like a crochet hook

pick up as many stitches as are necessary to avoid holes and then on the next row decrease to 95 sts for the back and 95 sts for the front.

Using the band needles rib in black 12 ply UNIQUE for 1 row.   *Rib 4 rows in the main 8 ply colour of your choice. Change to black and rib for 2 rows.*

Repeat this until there is a total of 4 bands of black and 4 of the main colour. Add 2 more rows of black and then cast off (bind off) evenly.

Cuffs

Repeat as for the bottom bands picking up as many sts as necessary to make a neat transition. Decrease on the next row to 37 sts for a very small cuff and 45 for a bigger one.

Neck Band

Sew one shoulder seam and use straight needles or sew both shoulder seams and use circular needles. Use the Up through the bar method for the seams.

Repeat the picking up method from the bottom band using black 12 ply but pick up as follows:

17 from the back of the neck, 17 from the cast on, 17 from the cast off, and 28 from the front curve of the neckhole (total 87 sts.)

Rib one row in black and 4 in the main colour then 10 rows in black. Cast off very

loosely. Sew neckband seam and remaining shoulder seam if necessary using the Up through the Bar method. Fold the band inwards and sew each stitch to its matching picked up stitch.

To Make Up

Sew the side seams using the Weaving method. Lay the edges of the fabric on a flat surface with the front side of the the fabric facing upwards. Use matching yarn to sew the seam. Illustration on page 126. Complete the sleeve seams the same way.

Setting in the sleeves

Sew to the body matching row for row.

Alternative Colourways

Three alternatives are shown but this design will adapt to many other colourways. Try green-blues with mint, or grey-blues with white and hot pink.

This design is effective as a coat. Add bands by continuing in rib on the same stitch numbers. Work pocket bands in the side seams. For full instructions see "EXTRA–Ordinarily You."

Key Design Elements

The key to the rich "Italian Style" fabric is the varied nature of the colours and yarns offset against the mathematically controlled ten stitch black bars which repeat every tenth stitch and every tenth row.

Corporate Spaces

The corporate world with its open offices and computer terminals is suggested in this structured but contemporary sweater.

Yarns Required

A: UNIQUE 8 ply
navy 409 x 7

B: ANGORA SUPREME
camel 1361 x 2 used
double

C: Cleckheaton COLLAGE
grey 1199 x 4

D: Any 8 ply cotton
light grey x 2
with any 8 ply cotton
taupe x 2

E: Lumpy cream cotton
embroidered on later or
knitted in

F: Any black 8 ply for
embroidery of small
lumps in centre of
squares of (D) x $1/4$

G: Any other lumpy
textured grey or black
yarns to be used in the
bands only x 1

Needles

3.5 mm (U.S. #4, U.K. #9)
for bands, cuff and
neckband

4.5 mm (U.S. #6, U.K. #7)
for body

Tension or Gauge

stocking stitch (stockinette)
20 sts and 28 rows to 10 cm
(4 inches)

Garment Size

Width: 63 cm (25")
Body stitches = 120
Length: 65 cm (25 $1/2$")
Total rows = 180

Back Band

Begin and end the band
with 3 rows of (A.)

Cast on loosely 90 sts in (A)
using the band needles.

Work the band in rib in
random colours for 24 rows
using (A) and (C) and (G)
but excluding (D) and (E).

On the next back facing
row: purl in (A) increasing
to 120 sts.

Change to body needles and

begin the graph

Work the textures as
follows:

A: Work all of (A) in
stocking stitch (knit the
front facing row and purl
the back facing row.)

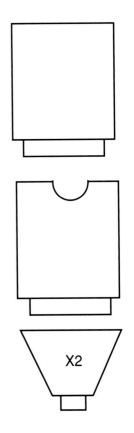

Corporate Spaces

Repeat between the arrows

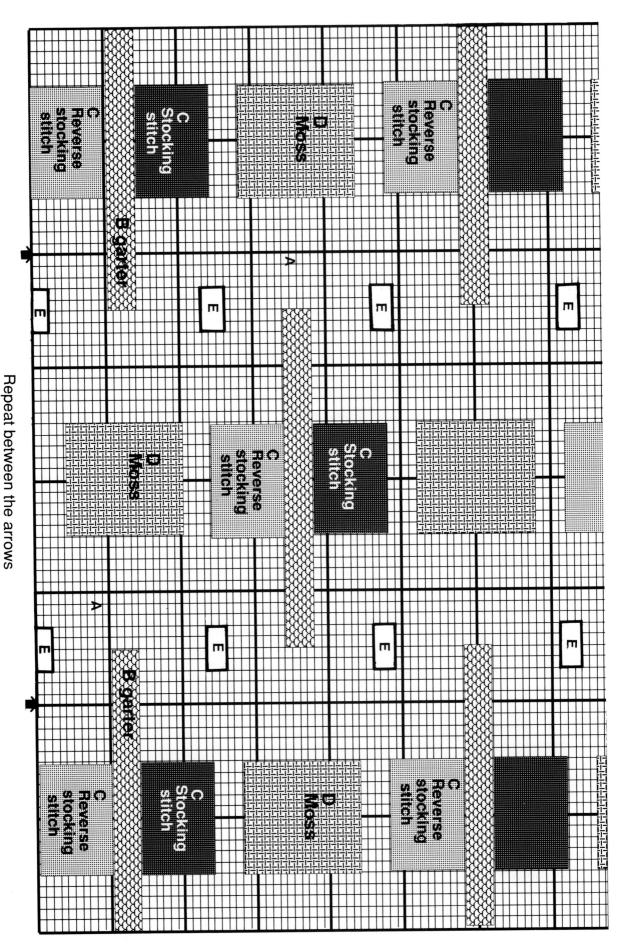

B: Work the first row of (B) in knit (front facing rows.)

Work the second, third and fourth rows of (B) in moss (or seed stitch.)

(K1, P1 and on the row back K the P and P the K)

or work (B) in garter stitch (knit every row.)

C: Work the block of (C) below the stripe of (B) in reverse stocking stitch but work the first row as normal stocking stitch.

Work the block of (C) above the stripe of (B) in normal stocking stitch.

D: Work (D) using the two soft cottons together in moss stitch but work the first row in stocking stitch.

E: Embroider (E) using duplicate stitch or swiss darning later or knit them in stocking stitch.

F: Embroider on small lumps of black at the end in the centres of the blocks of (D.)

G: Use only in the bands, cuffs and neckbands, in ribbing.

Read the graph beginning from the bottom right corner and read left for the first row and right for the second. Repeat between the arrows.

Use a separate ball every time a new colour appears. Work with a ball on either side of each block.

Hint for Intarsia

When you join in each of the new colours tie a neat knot and leave 10 cm (4 ") tails. Weave these in each stitch at the back while that colour lasts on the graph then leave them till the next row if necessary. If the width of the new colour is too narrow to use this method leave the tail and sew it in later along the edge of the colour change.

There is no armhole shaping for a drop shoulder style and no neck shaping on the back.

After three moss stitch blocks and three sets of (C) cast off (bind off) loosely in the matching colours.

Front

As for the back but this time shape the hole for the neck at the beginning of the last set of (C).

Put the central 10 sts on a holder or a safety pin. This will make it easier to pick up for the neckband and will help make the neck elastic. Decrease one each side every row for 10 rows until 45 sts remain on each shoulder.

Continue straight until the set of (C) is finished and the front matches the back in length. Cast off loosely matching the colours.

Sleeve

Cast on loosely 40 stitches using the band needles. Rib as for the bottom band. Then increase on a purl row evenly to 50 stitches using the body needles.

Continue as body graph, increasing one stitch each edge every 4th row.

When the sleeve is long enough cast off very loosely. The average sleeve is 50 cms in length.

Neck Band

Sew one shoulder seam using the Weaving method. Use straight needles and make a seam or sew both shoulders and use round needles or four needles.

Using a "band" needle like a crochet hook, (A) or the yarn which matches the top of the garment, face the front of the work and knit up stitches evenly around the hole as follows:

30 from the back of the neck, 13 along the straight vertical edge, 12 along the diagonal, knit the 10 from the safety pin to carry the yarn with you, then 12 and then 13 (total= 90 stitches.)

To avoid holes in the corners ignore that space and pick up stitches from either side of it.

Rib as for the band but put 8 rows of (A) in the middle to make the edge when the neckband is folded in.

77

and reinforce the first few stitches. Sew up to the ties at the arm pits. Reinforce again.

Setting in the sleeves

Alternate every stitch using the Weaving method for the sleeve stitches and the Up through the Bar method for the body rows.

Five stitches from the sleeve will match seven rows from the body as for any drop shoulder garment.

Check the inside for any remaining tails and sew these in along the edges of the colour change using a large eyed needle.

Alternative Colourways

The original is in navy with camel and charcoal and grey. Also shown is a reversed version of the same colours. The camel version used UNIQUE 8 ply camel 401 as the main yarn (A.)

For a major change in energy level, work with a red background, change the grey to princess blue and maintain the navy and charcoal.

For an even younger and more energetic effect work with all primary colours (red, yellow and blue.)

Key Design Elements

The textured yarns in the bands add the interest to this otherwise very conservative design.

Cast off (bind off) very loosely in rib.

Sew the remaining shoulder seam. Sew the band seam using the Up through the Bar method. Fold inwards and sew each stitch to its matching picked up stitch. Sew loosely to allow for stretch.

To Make Up

This should be done from the outside using two different techniques: Weaving and Up through the Bar.

Sew the sleeve seams including the ribbed bands using the Up through the Bar method. Reinforce the beginning of the cuff.

Lay the garment flat and find the armpit by stretching the cast off (bind off) row of the sleeve as deep as possible (at least 28 cms or 11 inches from the shoulder seam.) Tie the front to the back at this point on both sides of the body.

Side seams

Use the Up through the Bar method for both the ribbed bands and the stocking stitch (stockinette) side seams. Begin at the band

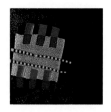

Computer Chips

Computer parts are fascinating in appearance quite apart from the the world of activity inside each one. The design image, an abstracted computer chip, repeats with variations. This principle of design (repetition with variations) is one of the most basic in contemporary design. Another basic principle of design (proportion of colour) is also used. The smaller blocks are brighter than the larger blocks.

Yarns Required

A: UNIQUE 12 ply
   black 507 x 8
   (background)

B: Cleckheaton
   SENSATION
   1271 x 4
   (large blocks)

C: Any hot pink cotton
   8 ply and red rayon
   8 ply together x 1
   (little blocks)

D: UNIQUE 12 ply
   princess blue 510 x1
   (little blocks)

E: Cleckheaton COLLAGE
   grey 1199 x $^1/2$
   (tiny blocks in
   background)

F: Green silk tweed or any
   other light blue–green
   yarn
   (embroidered slashes)

Yarns Required
Matching garments on male and female

A: UNIQUE 12 ply
    petral 511 x 8

B: UNIQUE 12 ply
    purple 508 x 3

C: UNIQUE 12 ply
   melon 512 x 1

D: UNIQUE 12 ply
   gold 504 x 1

E & F: UNIQUE 12 ply
   lilac 513 x 1

Needles

5 mm (U.S.#7, U.K.#6)
   needles for the bands,
   cuff and neckband.
6 mm (U.S.#9, U.K.#4)
   needles for the body.

Tension or Gauge
stocking stitch (stockinette)
17 sts and 22 rows
to l0 cm (4 inches)

Garment Size
Width: 52 cm or 20$^1/2$"
   (55 cm or 21$^1/2$", 58 cm
   or 23")
Total stitches = 88 (94, 100)

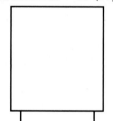

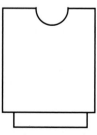

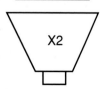

X2

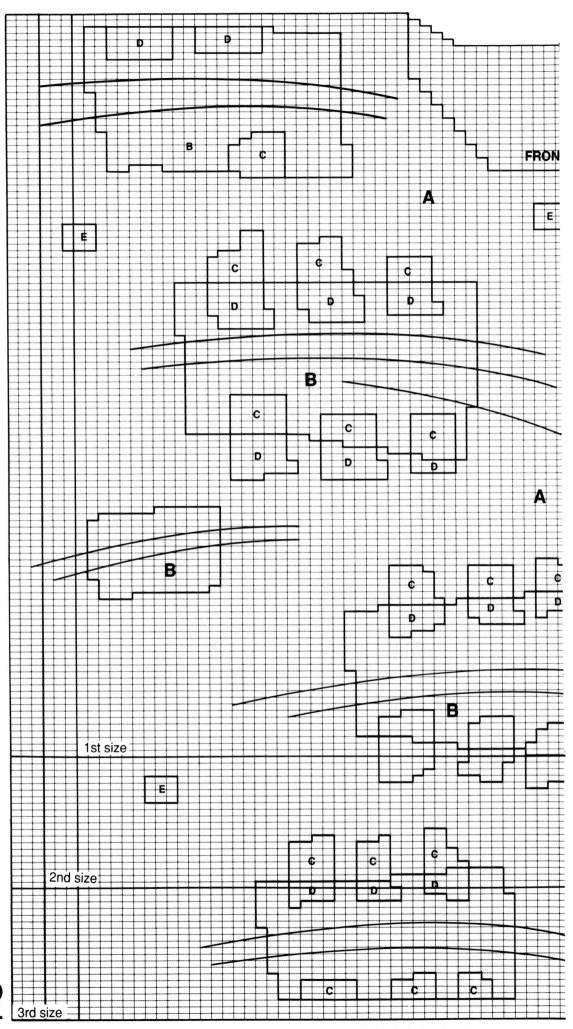

FRON

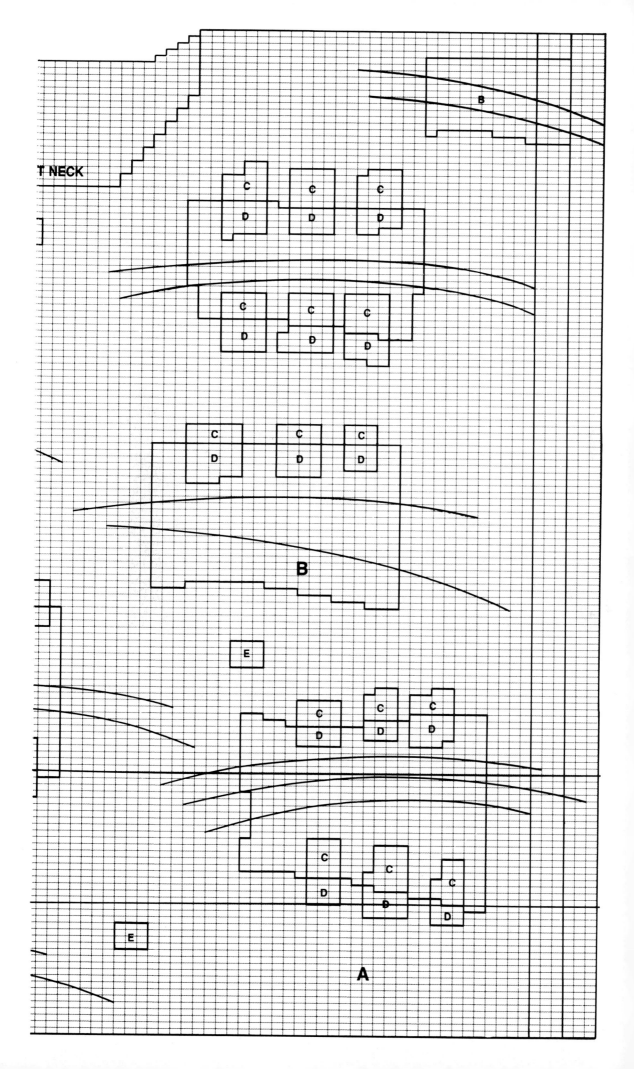

85

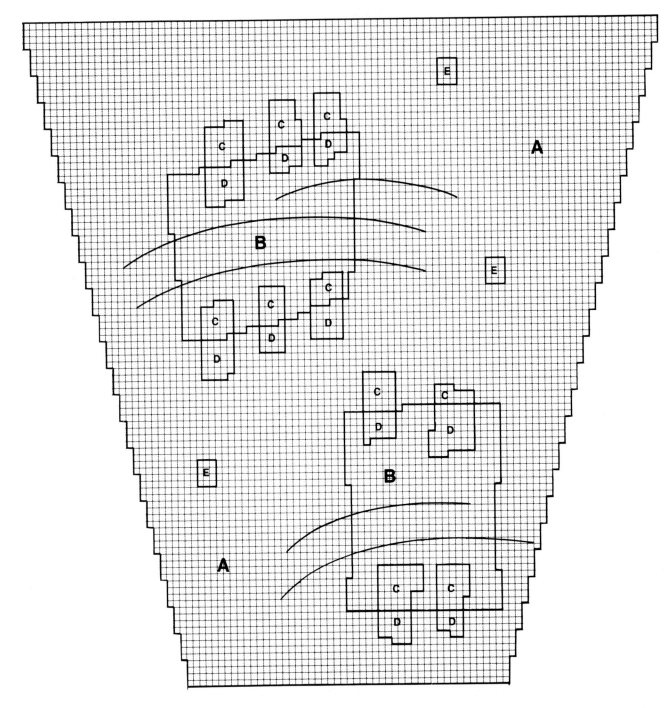

Length: 60 cm or 23¹/2", (70 cm or 27¹/2", 80 cm or 31¹/2")

Total rows = 138 (158, 178)

Back Band

Cast on loosely 80 (90, 100) sts using the band needles in (A.) Work the band for a total of 25 rows in rib.

Change to the body needles and do a purl row increasing to 90 (100, 120) sts evenly across the row. Begin the graph.

Reading a Graph

One stitch is represented by one square. Read from the bottom right hand corner to the left for the first knit row. Take special care for the first row because it establishes the position of all stitches above it.

Read from left to right for the purl row even though

you will still be knitting from right to left. Turn the graph upside down if it helps.

Completing the back

There is no armhole shaping for a drop shoulder style. Shape the neck hole on the back as indicated on the graph.

Cast off (bind off) loosely straight across the last row .

Front

As for the back but this time shape the hole for the neck as shown on the graph:

24 rows from the end divide the two shoulders by putting the 16 central stitches on a stitch holder or a safety pin. Decrease one stitch every 2nd row for 14 rows (seven decreases in all).

Continue straight for 10 rows. Cast off.

Sleeve

Both sleeves are the same. Do not mirror image them. Cast on 35 stitches using the band needles. Work the band as for the bottom back band. Change to the body needles. Increase on a purl row evenly to 50 stitches using the body needles.

Use the graph and increase one stitch each edge every 4th row. When the sleeve is long enough cast off very loosely. The average sleeve will end after the 95th row of the graph.

Neck Band

Sew one shoulder seam using the Weaving method. Using a "band" needle like a crochet hook, (A) coloured yarn and facing the front of the work knit up stitches evenly around the hole as follows: 28 from the back of the neck, 10 along the straight vertical edge, 14 along the diagonal, knit the 16 from the safety pin to carry the yarn with you, then 14 and then 10. (Total= 92 stitches)

Rib for 25 rows. Cast off (bind off) very loosely in rib using a "body" needle if necessary. Sew the neckband seam using the Up through the Bar method and the remaining shoulder seam using the Weaving method.

Fold the neckband inside. Sew each stitch down to its matching "picked up" stitch but make the loops slightly loose to allow the neck to stretch.

Sewing Up

This should be done from the outside using two different techniques: Weaving and Up through the Bar.

Sew the sleeve seams including the ribbed bands using the Up through the Bar method. Reinforce the beginning of the cuff.

Side seams

Use the Up through the Bar method for both the ribbed bands and the stocking stitch (stockinette) side seams. Begin at the band and reinforce the first few stitches. Sew side seams to within 28 cm (11") of shoulder seam. Reinforce again.

Setting in the sleeves

Alternate every stitch using the Weaving method for the sleeve stitches and the Up through the Bar method for the body rows.

Five stitches from the sleeve will match seven rows from the body as for any drop shoulder garment.

Check the inside for any remaining tails and sew these in along the edges of the colour change using a large eyed needle.

Alternative Colourways

The safest choice is to keep the background the darkest colour and the middle sized blocks in the middle range and the smallest blocks in the brightest colours of all. For example, use a navy background, mid blue for the middle sized blocks and a light blue and white for the smallest blocks.

Key Design Elements

Repetition is comforting because it is predictable. Difference is challenging because it is not. By repeating the abstracted computer chips in a range of slightly different formats, order is balanced against excitement.

Giant Cables

Simple oversized cables change colour on their way up the sweater. These braided ropes are created by crossing sets of stitches which pull the colours of the central panel into the strong simple curves of the cables. The cables begin with the coolest and darkest of the colours at the bottom and become warmer and brighter up towards the shoulders.

The outsides of the centre panel are plain so the attention is guided to the textured yarns and rich colour of the cables and the centre panel. The neckband and tops of the drop shoulder sleeves are also cabled separately and added later. This garment combines intarsia and aran techniques.

Yarns Required

A: CHANSON
    black 912 x 10

B: Cleckheaton
    NATURAL 12 ply
    Charcoal 1032 x 2

C: Cleckheaton COLLAGE
    red 1208 x 2

D: Cleckheaton
    SENSATION
    black 1271 x 2

E: Cleckheaton
    SENSATION
    red 1275 x 2

F: Any additional 12 ply
    yarn to make an extra
    cable set if required

G: Cleckheaton COLLAGE
    blue 1198 x 1

Special note
If you wish to change the colours of this design keep the cables and centre panels in the brighter or lighter colours and the background in the darker or cooler colours. This will encourage the cables to rise strongly above the surface of the background.

Needles
5 mm (U.S.#7, U.K.#6)
    needles for the bands,
    cuff and neckband.
6.5 mm (U.S.#10, U.K.#3)
    needles for the body.

Tension or Gauge
stocking stitch (stockinette)
13 sts and 20 rows
to 10 cm (4 inches)

Garment Size
Body Width: 61 cm or 24"

Stitch numbers = 100

Total Length: 60 cm or
    23$^{1}/_{2}$" (another cable set
    will make 70 cm or
    27$^{1}/_{2}$")

Row numbers = 138 or any
    additional 26 rows

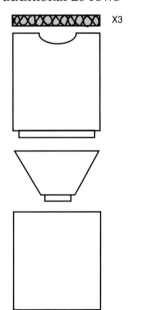

89

To increase the width

Halve the extra stitches that you need and add them onto either side of the outside panels. The design will not be effected because it is centred on the body. It will handle an indefinite number of increased stitches.

This garment combines intarsia and aran techniques. The basic concept will also adapt into a coat or cardigan.

Back

Cast on loosely 80 sts using the band needles. Work the band in rib using colour (A) for 20 rows.

Change to the body needles and do a purl row increasing to 90 sts evenly across the row.

You are now ready to begin adding in the colours for the cables.

Use a separate ball every time a new colour appears.

Hint for Intarsia

When you join in each of the new colours tie a neat knot and leave 10 cm (4") tails. Weave these in each stitch at the back while that colour lasts on the graph then leave them till the next row if necessary.

If the width of the new colour is too narrow to use this method leave the tail and sew it in later along the edge of the colour change.

First front facing row

Keep the background yarn (A) from the band attached and knit 30 sts. Tie on (B) and knit 5 sts using only 3 three sts from the band, tie on (G) and knit 5 sts using only 2 sts from the band, carry (B) loosely behind and knit 20 for the central panel. Tie on another ball of (G) and knit 5 using only 2 sts from the band. Carry (B) loosely behind and knit 5 using only 3 from the band. Tie on another ball of (A) and knit to the end of the row (30 sts.)

ROW 2: Purl the next row crossing over the yarns in between the colour change but working the same colours as the row below.

ROW 3: Knit 30 in (A). Put the next 5 sts of (B) on a cable needle and hold to the back. Knit 5 (G) in (G), K 5 (B) off the cable needle in (B), knit 20 (B) in (B). Put the next 5 (G) onto a cable needle and hold to the front, knit 5 (B) in (B), knit 5 (G) off the cable needle in (C), knit 30 in (A.)

ROW 4: as row 2

Continue for 8 rows after the cable row in stocking stitch (stockinette) matching the colours with the row below.

ROW 11: Using (A) knit 25, put the next 5 sts of (A) on a cable needle and pass to the back. Cross (A) over (G). Knit the next 5 sts of (G) with (G). Knit the 5 (A) sts off the cable needle with (A). Put the next 5 sts of (B) onto a cable needle and hold them to the front. Knit the next 5 (B) sts in (A). Knit the (B) sts off the cable needle in (B). Continue knitting in (B) for the next 10 sts. Put the next 5 sts of (B) on a cable needle and hold to the back. Knit the next 5 (B) sts in (B). Knit the 5 (B) sts off the cable needle using a second ball of (A). Put the next 5 (G) sts on the cable needle and hold them to the front. Knit the next 5 sts of (A) in (A). Knit the 5 sts off the cable needle in (G). Continue the row in (A) for the remaining 25 sts.

ROW 12: Purl working with the colours from the row below.

Continue for 10 rows working in stocking stitch (stockinette) using the colours from the row below.

ROW 21: Using (A) knit 25. Put the next 5 sts of (G) on a cable needle and hold to the front. Knit the next 5 sts of (A) with (A). Knit the 5 sts of (G) off the cable needle with (G). Put the next 5 sts of (A) onto a cable needle and and hold them to the back. Knit the next 5 sts of (B) with (B). Knit the 5 (A) sts off the cable needle in (B.)

Knit the central 10 sts of (B) with (B). Put the next 5 sts on to a cable needle, hold to the front. Knit 5 (B) with

(B), knit 5 off the cable needle with (B), put 5 (A) onto a cable needle and hold them to the back. Knit the next 5 (G) in (G) crossing the yarns over, knit 5 off the cable needle in (A). Knit 25 in (A.)

ROW 22: Purl using the colours from the row below.

Continue for a further 6 rows (8 altogether.)

This completes one set of 26 rows (plus the two extra rows at the beginning of the back to establish the cable).

Begin the next set:

ROW 1: Using (A) knit 30. Put the next 5 sts of (G) on a cable needle and hold to the back. Knit the next 5 sts of (B) with (B). Cut (G) and tie on (C). Knit the 5 sts of (G) off the cable needle with (C). Continue across the row in (C) (20 sts). Put the next 5 sts of (B) on the cable needle and hold to the front. Cut off (G) and tie the tail to a new (B). Knit the next 5 sts of (G) with (C). Knit the 5 sts of (B) off the cable needle using (B). Finish the row (30 sts) in (A).

ROW 2: Purl using the colours from the row below.

Continue for 8 rows in stocking stitch (stockinette).

Cable to bring (A) into the centre of the cable. Continue for a total of 10 rows.

Close the cable.

Continue for a total of 8 rows.

Begin the next set using (C) for the outside cables and introducing (D) for the centre.

Complete the 26 pattern rows .

Begin the next set using (D) for the outside cable and using (E) for the centre.

If this is to be the last set then do not cable after the introduction row.

Continue straight for 26 rows using the colours from the first row of the set. This allows the top to get wider than the bottom of the sweater and adds width over the shoulder area as all 100 sts come into play.

There is no armhole shaping for a drop shoulder style and no neck shaping on the back.

Cast off (bind off) straight across the last row loosely so the shoulders will stretch comfortably. Use the colours from the row below.

Front

As for the back but this time shape the hole for the neck as follows:

After 8 rows of the last set have been completed divide the two shoulders by putting the 10 central

stitches on a stitch holder or a safety pin. This will make it easier to pick up for the neckband and will help make the neck elastic. Decrease one each neck edge, every row for 10 rows.

Continue straight for 8 rows.

Cast off maintaining the colours.

Sleeve

The design for the sleeves is the effect of the two cables from the front overlaid and the central panel eliminated altogether.

Cast on 35 sts using (A) and the band needles. Rib for 20 rows.

Increase on a purl row evenly to 50 sts using the body needles.

ROW 1: (First front facing row) Keep the background yarn (A) attached and knit 20 sts. Tie on (G) and knit 5 sts, tie on (B) and knit 5 sts, carry loosely behind and knit in (A) to the end of the row.

Purl the next row crossing over the yarns inbetween the colour change but working with the same colours as the row below.

Continue for 4 rows total.

Increase one st each edge on the next knit row and continue for a further three rows.

ROW 9: Using (A) increase one, K15, put the next 5 sts of (A) on a cable needle and pass to the back. Knit the next 5 sts of (G) with (G). Knit the 5 (A) sts with (A). Put the next 5 sts of (B) onto a cable needle and hold them to the front. Knit the next 5 (A) sts in (A). Knit the (B) sts off the cable needle in (B.)

Continue the row in (A) for the remaining 15 sts then increasing one at the end of the row.

Continue the design established using the same rows for cabling and the same rows for the colour changes as established in the body.

When the sleeve is 50 cm long or the desired length (less the extra sideways cable) cast off (bind off.)

Sideways Cable

Make three lengths of cable to use at the top of the sleeves and for the neckband.

Using colour (E) and the body needles cast on 12 sts. stocking stitch for 6 rows. On the next front facing row K1, cable the next 10 sts (5 over 5 in any direction), K1.

Stocking stitch for 13 rows, cable again.

Repeat this pattern for a total of 9 cables and then work 5 rows in stocking stitch. Graft the last row to the first to make a ring.

Sew one ring to the top of each sleeve and the third one as the neckband.

Sewing Up

This should be done from the outside using two different techniques: Weaving and Up through the Bar.

Sew the sleeve seams including the ribbed bands using the Up through the Bar method.

Reinforce the beginning of the cuff as this will be under a lot of stress over the years.

Sew the shoulder seams using the Weaving method loosely. Illustration on page 126.

Side seams

Use the Up through the Bar method for both the ribbed bands and the stocking stitch (stockinette) side seams. Begin at the band and reinforce the first few stitches. Sew side seams to within 28 cm (11") of shoulder seam. Reinforce again.

Setting in the sleeves

Stretch the cable ring in (E) as deep as possible and set into the side seam of the body.

Check the inside for any remaining tails and sew these in along the edges of the colour change using a large eyed needle.

Alternative Colourways

The original has black sides and ranges from charcoal to rust–red in the centre.

Alternatives would be:

black sides and a range of charcoal to silver–grey in the centre

navy sides and a range of charcoal to mid–blue in the centre

charcoal sides and a range of mid–blue to lilac in the centre

olive sides and a range of brick to light rust in the centre

black sides and blue, purple, red, red–gold in the centre

black sides and dark jade–green, blue, red–gold in the centre.

Start dark and get lighter or start cooler and get warmer. (Warmer colours have more yellow or red in them.)

Key Design Elements

The keys are the dark sides and the graded nature of the colour changes in the centre.

The cables combine the colours from both the central panel immediately below and the current central panel.

The colour of the outside panels is integrated into the centre panel by appearing through the gap created by the curves of the cables.

93

Silk Leaves

Warm coloured, silky leaves in random shapes float across the surface of the central panel.
Black stalks curl out from each leaf forming their own relationships..
The bottom band, cuffs and neck are in a textured stitch which encourages the boxy contemporary shape.

Yarns Required
A: UNIQUE 8 ply
    gray 418 x 7
B: UNIQUE 8 ply
    lilac 413 x 4
Plus 100 gms of mixed
    yarns for leaves

Needles
4 mm (U.S.#5, U.K.#8)
    needles for the bottom
    bands, cuffs and
    neckband
5 mm (U.S.#7, U.K. #6)
    needles for the body

Tension or Gauge
stocking stitch (stockinette)
19 sts and 25 rows
to 10 cm (4 inches)

Garment Size
Body width: 60 cm or 23^1/$_2$"
    (70 cm or 27^1/$_2$", 80 cm or
    31^1/$_2$")

Stitch numbers = 110,(132, 156)
Total Length: 60 cm or
    23^1/$_2$", (65 cm or 25^1/$_2$",
    70 cm or 27^1/$_2$")
Row numbers = 166 (180, 192)
Any combination can be made depending on your needs.

To increase the width
Halve the extra stitches that you need and add them onto either side of the outside panels.

Use the background colour that appears on that side. The design will not be effected because it is centred on the body.

Back
Cast on loosely 90 (110, 130 sts) using (A) and the band needles. Work the band pattern as follows:

Band pattern
ROW 1: Knit 2, purl 2 across the row to the last 2 sts then knit 2.

Repeat row 1 for a total of 31 rows.

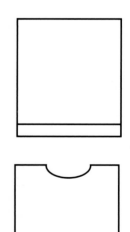

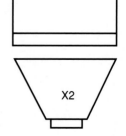

X2

95

Change to the body needles and do a purl row increasing to 110 (132, 156) sts evenly across the row. Work the first 36 (44, 56) sts in colour (A) then the centre panel of 38 (44, 44) sts in (B) and the remaining 36 (44, 44) sts in (A) again using a separate ball.

Add in the new colours for the leaves as necessary leaving the background yarns attached. Use a separate ball of background yarn on the other side of the leaf.

Make up leaf shapes using the graph as a guide only. No two leaf shapes need be the same. Repeat the same shape in a different colour or repeat the colour in a different shape.

Read the graph beginning from the bottom right corner and read left for the first row and right for the second. You may find it easier to tip the graph upside down to read every second row if you are not very experienced.

Hint for Intarsia

When you join in each of the new colours tie a neat knot and leave 10 cm (4 ") tails. Weave these in each stitch at the back while that colour lasts on the graph then leave them till the next row if necessary. If the width of the new colour is too narrow to use this method leave the tail and sew it in later along the edge of the colour change.

If making textured leaves, work the first and outside stitches in stocking stitch.

There is no armhole shaping for a drop shoulder and no neck shaping at the back of this garment. Work until the back is long enough then cast off loosely.

Front

As back until neck shaping. Shape the neck on the front as follows:

Work until the front is 30 rows shorter than the back (12 cm or 5 inches.) Put the central 20 sts on a holder. Add the background yarn to the side without yarn and work both sides at once.

Decrease one each neck edge each front facing row for a total of 10 rows. (This makes five decreases each side.) Continue straight for 20 rows. Cast off (bind off) straight across the last row loosely so the shoulders will stretch comfortably.

Sleeve

Cast on loosely 36 stitches using (A) and the band needles. Work the band pattern for 30 rows. Increase on a purl row evenly to 54 (60, 60) stitches using the body needles. Keep the centre 38 (44, 44) sts in (B) colour and the remaining outside sts in (A.)

Continue in stocking stitch

(stockinette) increasing one stitch each edge every 4th row.

To match the increases for sewing the sleeve seam knit into the front and then the back of the first stitch. Complete the row till two stitches remain. Knit into the front and then the back of the next stitch, knit the last stitch.

When the sleeve is long enough (approximately 50 cm) cast off very loosely.

Neck Band

Sew one shoulder seam using the Weaving method. Illustration on page 126.

Using a "band" needle like a crochet hook and the band yarn or the yarn which matches the top of the garment, face the front of the work and knit up stitches evenly around the hole as follows: 30 from the back of the neck, 17 along the straight vertical edge, 8 along the diagonal, knit the 20 from the safety pin to carry the yarn with you, then 8 and then 17 (total 100 sts.) To avoid holes in the corners ignore that space and pick up stitches from either side of it.

Work the band pattern for 30 rows. Cast off (bind off) very loosely in rib.

Sew the remaining shoulder seam. Sew the neck band seam using the Up through the Bar method.

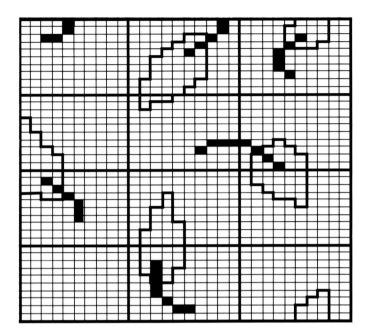

Fold the neckband inside and sew each stitch to its matching picked up stitch loosely to allow for stretch.

To Make Up

This should be done from the outside using two different techniques: Weaving and Up through the Bar.

Sew the sleeve seams including the ribbed bands using the Up through the Bar method. Reinforce the beginning of the cuff.

Lay the garment flat and find the armpit by stretching the cast off (bind off) row of the sleeve as deep as possible. This should be at least 28 cm or 11 inches from the shoulder seam.

Tie the front to the back at this point on both sides of the body.

Side seams

Use the Up through the Bar method for both the ribbed bands and the stocking stitch (stockinette) side seams. Begin at the band and reinforce the first few stitches.

Sew up to the ties at the arm pits. Reinforce again.

Setting in the sleeves

Alternate every stitch using the Weaving method for the sleeve stitches and the Up through the Bar method for the body rows.

Five stitches from the sleeve will match seven rows from the body as for any drop shoulder garment.

Check the inside for any remaining tails and sew these in along the edges of the colour change using a large eyed needle, or extend the tip of the leaf.

Embroidery

Using black and a darning needle or crochet hook, work the stems of the leaves as desired, if they have not been knitted in.

Alternative Colourways

The suggested alternatives all have black stalks.

black outsides and grey centre with white and cream leaves

grey outsides and white centre with charcoal leaves

navy outsides and princess blue centre with saxe blue leaves

nut brown outsides with brown centre and camel and coffee leaves

olive outsides with brown centre and charcoal and red leaves

purple outsides with brick red centre and gold leaves

melon outsides with gold centre and olive leaves

Key Design Elements

The small line of black in each leaf is very important to hold the many variables in the leaves together. Black is the end of the line; a stopping point. As such, it provides the boundary for all the other colours.

The repetition of the leaf shape, floating on various angles, is a play on all 'repeat prints.'

Santa Fe

Navaho weavings, turquoise jewellery, and the colours of the desert combine in this design.

Yarns Required
A: ANGORA SUPREME
coffee 1361 x 7
B: UNIQUE 8 ply
cream 423 x 2
C: UNIQUE 8 ply
purple 408 x 2
D: UNIQUE 8 ply
black 407 x 1
E: UNIQUE 8 ply
gold 404 x 1
F: MOHAIR 90
neptune 888 x 1
G: UNIQUE 8 ply
brown 405 x 1
H: UNIQUE 8 ply
brick red 406 x 1
I: UNIQUE 8 ply
melon 412 x 1

Needles
3.5 mm (U.S.#4 U.K.#10)
needles for the bands,
cuff and neckband.
4 mm (U.S.#6 or U.K.#8)
needles for the body.

Tension or Gauge
stocking stitch (stockinette)
22 sts and 30 rows
to 10 cm (4 inches)

Garment Size
Body Width: 55 cm or
21^1/$_2$" (60 cm or 23^1/$_2$",
70 cm or 27^1/$_2$")
Stitch numbers = 120 (132,
154)
Total Length: 60 cm or
23^1/$_2$" (65 cm or 2^1/$_2$", 70
cms or 27^1/$_2$")
Row numbers = 180 (195,
210)

The graph shows the
smallest size in both width
and length but any
combinations may be made
depending on your needs.

To increase the width
Halve the extra stitches that
you need and add them
onto either side of the
graph. Work the extra
stitches in the main
background colour.

Back
Cast on loosely 100 (120,
140) sts using the band
needles and (A). Work the
band in rib for 25 rows.

Change to the body needles
and do a purl row
increasing to 120 (132,154)
sts evenly across the row.

You are now ready to begin
the graph in stocking stitch
(stockinette.)

Read the graph beginning
from the bottom right
corner and read left for the
first row and right for the
second. You may find it
easier to tip the graph
upside down to read every
second row if you are not
very experienced.

Use a separate ball every
time a new colour appears.

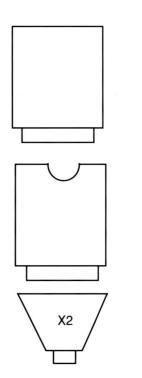

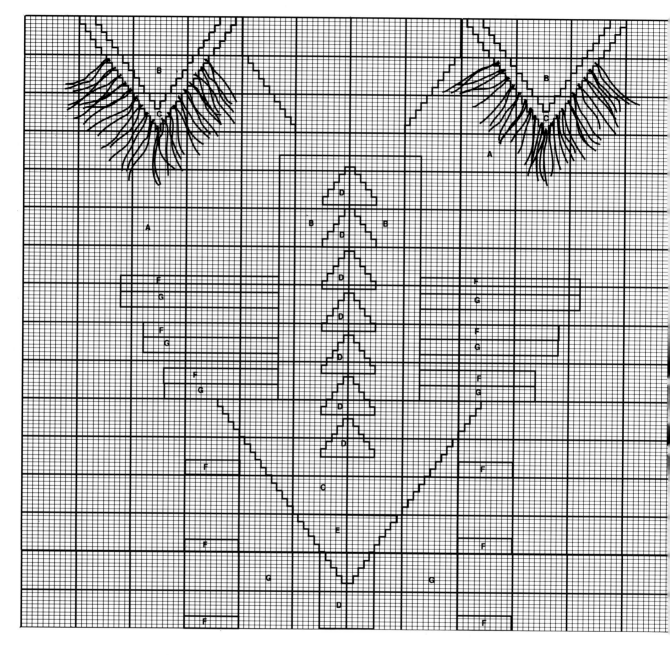

Hint for Intarsia

When you join in each of the new colours tie a neat knot and leave 10 cm (4") tails. Weave these in each stitch at the back while that colour lasts on the graph then leave them till the next row if necessary. If the width of the new colour is too narrow to use this method leave the tail and sew it in later along the edge of the colour change.

There is no armhole shaping for a drop shoulder style and no neck shaping on the back so continue the graph filling in the hole for the front neck shaping.

Cast off (bind off) straight across the last row loosely so the shoulders will stretch comfortably.

Front

As for the back but this time shape the hole for the neck as indicated on the graph. Divide the two shoulders by putting the 20 central stitches on a stitch holder or a safety pin. This will make it easier to pick up for the

Neck Band

Sew one shoulder seam using the Weaving method. Use straight needles and make a seam or sew both shoulders and use round needles or four needles.

Using a "band" needle like a crochet hook and the band yarn or the yarn which matches the top of the garment, face the front of the work and knit up stitches evenly around the hole as follows:

40 from the back of the neck, 8 along the straight vertical edge, 18 along the diagonal, knit the 20 from the safety pin to carry the yarn with you, then 18 and then 8. (Total=112 stitches) To avoid holes in the corners ignore that space and pick up stitches from either side of it.

Rib as for the band.

Cast off (bind off) very loosely in rib.

Sew the remaining shoulder seam. Sew the band seam using the Up through the Bar method and fold the neckband inwards and sew each stitch allowing for stretch.

To Make Up

This should be done from the outside using two different techniques: Weaving and Up through the Bar.

Sew the sleeve seams

---

neckband and will help make the neck elastic. Decrease one each side every row for 20 rows.

Continue straight for the remaining rows. Cast off loosely.

Sleeve

The sleeves are exactly the same as each other.

Cast on loosely 50 stitches using the band needles. Rib as for the bottom band. Then increase on a purl row evenly to 66 stitches using the body needles.

Continue in stocking stitch (stockinette) using the graph and increasing one stitch each edge every 4th row.

To match the increases for sewing the sleeve seam knit into the front and then the back of the first stitch. Complete the row till two stitches remain. Knit into the front and then the back of the next stitch, knit the last stitch.

When the sleeve is long enough (approximately 50 cm) cast off very loosely.

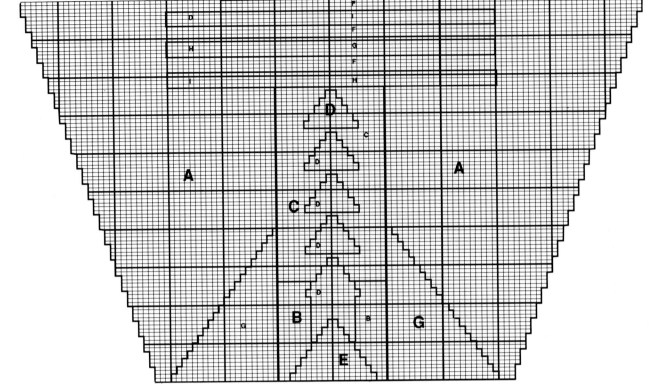

including the ribbed bands using the Up through the Bar method. Reinforce the beginning of the cuff.

Lay the garment flat and find the armpit by stretching the cast off (bind off) row of the sleeve as deep as possible (at least 28 cms or 11 inches from the shoulder seam.) Tie the front to the back at this point on both sides of the body.

Side seams
Use the Up through the Bar method for both the ribbed bands and the stocking stitch (stockinette) side seams. Begin at the band and reinforce the first few stitches. Sew up to the ties

at the arm pits. Reinforce again.

Setting in the sleeves
Alternate every stitch using the Weaving method for the sleeve stitches and the Up through the Bar method for the body rows.

Five stitches from the sleeve will match seven rows from the body as for any drop shoulder garment.

Check the inside for any remaining tails and sew these in along the edges of the colour change using a large eyed needle.

Alternative Colourways
The original is in desert colours with strong

highlights of turquoise. An alternative would be a black background with the same turquoise highlights. Replace the current black triangles with hot pink.

Key Design Elements
The influence of the mid west of the United States has infiltrated the world of fashion and architecture. The woven designs of the natives of the area provide the basic horizontal design.

More influencial again is the expanse of blue sky over the warm earth and the small adobe buildings which combine the colours of both. The colours of the earth and the sky are used in this design.

Slash and Dash

The striped patterning of the coloured bands in the background are cut across by the moving black slashes like dashing thoughts and fleeting ideas. These diagonals add movement and intention to the otherwise quiet, subtle colours.

Yarns Required

A: UNIQUE 8 ply
   cream 423 x 2
B: ANGORA SUPREME
   camel 1361 x 1
C: UNIQUE 8 ply
   mushroom 400 x 1
D: Cleckheaton NATURAL
   grey 1031 x 2
E: Cleckheaton NATURAL
   cream 1030 x 2
F: UNIQUE 8 ply
   gray 418 x 1
G: any lumpy cotton in a
   camel or cream
H: Shepherd
   THISTLEDOWN
   gold x 2
I: any light grey cotton x 1
J: ANGORA SUPREME
   white 1351 x $^1/_2$

Black slashes and bands
UNIQUE 8 ply
   black 407 x 4

The background is in sets of stripes with two rows per colour. Each colour is introduced as follows: AB AC, BC BD, CD CE, DE DF, EF EG, FG FH, GH GI, HI HJ, JA JB, AB AC, BC BE, CD CF etc.

Needles

3.5 mm (U.S.#4, U.K.#10)
   needles for the bands,
   cuff and neckband.
4 mm (U.S.#6, U.K.#8)
   needles for the body.

Tension or Gauge

stocking stitch (stockinette)
22 sts and 30 rows
to 10 cm (4 inches)

Garment Size

Body Width: 54 cm or
21" (60 cm or 23$^1/_2$"
Stitch numbers = 120 (132)
Total Length: 60 cm or
   23$^1/_2$" (65 cm or 2$^1/_2$",
   70 cm or 27$^1/_2$")
Row numbers = 180 (195,
   210)
Any combinations may be made depending on your needs.

To increase the width
Halve the extra stitches that you need and add them onto either side of the graph.

The graph shows the smallest width and length.

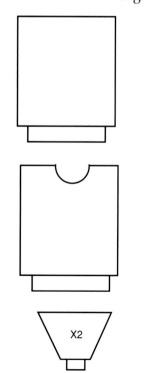

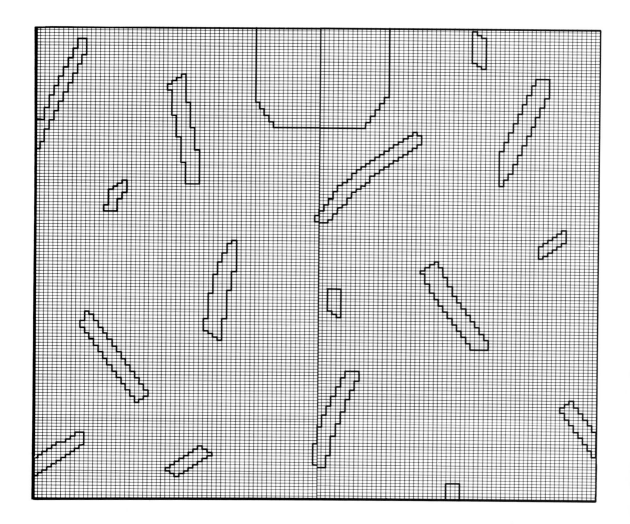

Back

Cast on loosely 100 (120) sts using the band needles. Work the band in rib for 20 rows in black.

Change to the body needles and do a purl row increasing to 110 (132) sts evenly across the row.

You are now ready to begin the graph in stocking stitch (or stockinette.)

Read the graph beginning from the bottom right corner and read left for the first row and right for the second. You may find it easier to tip the graph upside down to read every second row if you are not very experienced.

Use a separate length of black yarn for every slash.

Work the extra stitches required on the outside edges without slashes and work the extra rows required for any larger sizes after the band and at the beginning of the graph.

Work the black slashes in intarsia with a separate ball of yarn on either side of the slash if your fairisle technique is at all "questionable."

Hint for Intarsia

When you join in each of the new colours tie a neat knot and leave 10 cm (4") tails. Weave these in each stitch at the back while that colour lasts on the graph then leave them till the next row if necessary. If the width of the new colour is too narrow to use this method leave the tail and sew it in later along the edge of the colour change.

There is no armhole shaping for a drop shoulder style and no neck shaping on the back so continue the graph filling in the hole for the front neck shaping.

Cast off (bind off) straight across the last row loosely so the shoulders will stretch comfortably.

Front

As for the back but this time shape the hole for the neck 32 rows from the end as indicated on the graph. Divide the two shoulders by putting the 20 central stitches on a stitch holder or a safety pin. This will make it easier to pick up for the neckband and will help make the neck elastic. Decrease one each side every row for 10 rows.

Continue straight for 22 rows. Cast off loosely.

Sleeve

The sleeves are exactly the same as each other. Do not make them a mirror image.

Cast on loosely 40 stitches using the band needles. Rib as for the bottom band. Then increase on a purl row evenly to 60 stitches using the body needles.

Continue in stocking stitch (stockinette) using the central 60 sts of the graph and increasing one stitch each edge every 4th row.

When the sleeve is long enough cast off very loosely.

The average sleeve is 50 cms in length.

Neck Band

Sew one shoulder seam using the Weaving method.

Using a "band" needle like a crochet hook and the band yarn or the yarn which matches the top of the garment, face the front of the work and knit up stitches evenly around the hole as follows:

30 from the back of the neck, 18 along the straight vertical edge, 13 along the diagonal, knit the 20 from the safety pin to carry the yarn with you, then 13 and then 18. (Total=112 stitches) To avoid holes in the corners ignore that space and pick up stitches from either side of it.

Rib as for the band.

Cast off (bind off) very loosely in rib.

Sew the remaining shoulder seam. Sew the band seam using the Up through the Bar method. Fold inwards and sew down each stitch allowing for stretch.

To Make Up

This should be done from the outside using two different techniques: Weaving and Up through the Bar.

Sew the sleeve seams including the ribbed bands using the Up through the

Bar method. Reinforce the beginning of the cuff.

Lay the garment flat and find the armpit by stretching the cast off (bind off) row of the sleeve as deep as possible (at least 28 cm or 11 inches from the shoulder seam.) Tie the front to the back at this point on both sides of the body.

Side seams

Use the Up through the Bar method for both the ribbed bands and the stocking stitch (stockinette) side seams. Begin at the band and reinforce the first few stitches. Sew up to the ties at the arm pits. Reinforce again.

Setting in the sleeves

Alternate every stitch using the Weaving method for the sleeve stitches and the Up through the Bar method for the body rows.

Five stitches from the sleeve will match seven rows from the body as for any drop shoulder garment.

Check the inside for any remaining tails and sew these in along the edges of the colour change using a large eyed needle.

Alternative Colourways

Use a range of 10 similar colours in a similar weight (8 ply or DK.) The original is in soft, sandy colours reminiscent of the desert. The black is the strong contrast.

Any set of colours which are closely related will work.

The best effects will be achieved by choosing colours which would all photograph as similar greys on black and white film.

The general feeling can be changed to cooler, or warmer, or darker, or brighter.

Try all mid blues and mid greens and mid purples
or soft golds and milky coffees and soft pinks
or pale blues, pale lilacs and pale pinks
or soft greys and grey blues and lilacs
or reds, purple and plums.

Choosing different coloured background yarns
If you prefer a softer rolling look to the colours then choose a colour which is close to the one you have been using to swop to. A colour is "close" if it is similar in colour but slightly different in darkness or lightness (monochromatic colours.)

Two yarns are also "close" if they are a different colour but the same darkness or lightness and of similar "value." These make rolling waves.

Another alternative is to work with analogous colours. To find analogous colours, choose from within 90 degrees on the colour wheel and within the same circle.

Remember, if you want to flatter the physique (or figure) then work with predominantly darker, cooler colours at the bottom and gradually introduce lighter colours up towards the shoulders. This will lead the eye up to the chest and shoulders and also make them look bigger.

Key Design Elements
The strong contrast between the background and the slashes creates the tonal interest. The changing directions of the slashes provides the graphic interest.

Lightening

Repetitive zig zag lines are individually worked in mohair along with random coloured rows of mixed yarns to create a balance between patterning and freedom.
The current background yarn is carried behind but each zig zag is a separate strand. Extra, hot pink flashes, appear at random.

Yarns Required

Background yarns

UNIQUE 8 ply
    princess blue 410 x 5
    (for bands and body)
UNIQUE 8 ply
    bottle 422 x 2
UNIQUE 8 ply
    petral 411 x 2
UNIQUE 8 ply
    purple 408 x 1
UNIQUE 8 ply
    navy 409 x 1
UNIQUE 8 ply
    gray 418 x 1
UNIQUE 8 ply
    lilac 413 x 2
UNIQUE 8 ply
    saxe blue 421 x 1
Cleckheaton HIGHLAND
    navy 1132 x 1
Cleckheaton HIGHLAND
    lilac 1148 x 1

Zig zag yarns

CHANSON
    blue 905 x 1
CHANSON
    jade 904 x 1
MOHAIR 90
    perfect blue 890 x 1
MOHAIR 90
    neptune 888 x1
Eagle RENOIR
    purple (with hot pink
    spots) x 2

Flashes yarn

VAL DEVINE'S random
    dyed bouclé hot to soft
    pink x 50 gms or
Cleckheaton NOSTALGIA
    hot pink 1502 x 1

Cut into 25 lengths, 50 cm (20") long for the front and back, and another 20 lengths for the sleeves as desired.

Needles

3.5 mm (U.S.#4, U.K.#8)
    needles for the bands,
    cuff and neckband
4.5 mm (U.S.#6,U.K.#7)
    needles for the body.

Tension or Gauge

stocking stitch (stockinette)
20 sts and 24 rows to l0 cm (4 inches)

Garment Size

Width: 68 cm or 27"
Body stitches = 130 sts
Length: 70 cms or 27"
Total rows = 168 rows

To increase width

Add stitches in multiples of 10.

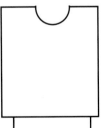

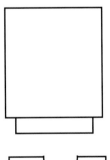

X2

109

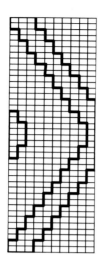

Three pattern concepts
1) Zig Zag graph
2) Background stripes
3) Flashes

1) Zig Zag Graph
To make the zig zag stand out you may wish to carry the main yarn across the back but use a different coloured ball of yarn for each zig zag. Use the MOHAIR 90 and the CHANSON for the zig zags. The colours can go in any order.

Read the graph beginning from the bottom right corner and read left for the first row and right for the second.

2) Background Stripes
Choose any of the background yarns and work in any order.

Carry the same yarn up the sides loosely for a few rows and use again if you like it. Cut off the colour when you know you don't want to work with it again for 10 rows or more and weave in the tail along the back, along with the tail of the new yarn. Do no more than ten rows of one colour. Change in the middle of the row or at the side...wherever you choose.

Work the RENOIR in as single or double rows only, and space throughout the garment for the best effect with just one ball.

3) Flashes
Work in flashes of hot pink randomly. Keep them in the centre thirty or so stitches but not immediately above the previous flash.

Cut the current background yarn and tie on a "flash" whenever you feel like it. When the "flash" yarn has run out, take the opportunity to change the background colour when tying on the next yarn.

Back
Cast on 120 stitches using the band needles and the band yarn (UNIQUE princess blue.) Work the band in rib for 30 rows. To do "Rib" knit 1, purl 1, across the row. If you end with a purl stitch begin the next row with a knit.

Change to the body needles and on the next back facing row purl increasing to 130 sts evenly across the row.

ROW 1: Begin the zig zag graph and one of the background colours. Tie on all of the zig zag yarns across the first row. Repeat the graph 13 times across the row.

Work the whole garment in stocking stitch (stockinette.)

Add in the first flash about 30 rows into the body. They can appear more frequently up towards the face and more frequently again for a female.

There is no armhole shaping for a drop shoulder style and no neck shaping on the back. Work until the garment is as long as required. Cast off (bind off) straight across the last row loosely so the shoulders will stretch comfortably.

Front
Work as back until the front measures 24 rows (10 cm or 4") shorter than the back.

Put the centre 16 sts on a holder. Cast off (bind off) 2 sts at the beginning of each neck edge 5 times. Continue straight on each front until it is the same length as the back. Cast off loosely the remaining 48 sts on each shoulder.

Sleeve
Cast on loosely 40 sts using the band needles. Rib for 25 rows. Increase on a purl row evenly to 50 sts using the body needles.

Continue in stocking stitch (stockinette). Begin by repeating the graph five times across the row. Also increase one stitch each edge every 4th row but do not add in any more zig zags.

The "flash" yarn can positioned anywhere on the sleeves.

When the sleeve is long enough cast off very loosely. The average length is 53 cm or 21 inches. Remember the length required is dictated by the width of the knitted body of the garment not just by the length of the arm of the recipient.

If a more fitted sleeve is desired stop increasing after the elbow (or at any point) and go straight.

If a deeper batwing sleeve to the waist is required increase every 2nd row rather than every 4th.

Neck Band

Sew the shoulder seam using the Weaving method. Using the "band" needle like a crochet hook face the front of the work. Starting at the left shoulder seam pick up and knit 10 sts from the straight part of the front, 10 sts from the diagonal, 16 from the front holder, 10 from the other diagonal, 10 from the remaining front edge and 36 from the back of the neck (total 92 sts.)

To avoid holes in the corners ignore that space and pick up stitches from either side of it.

Rib for 30 rows. Cast off (bind off) evenly but loosely in rib using a "body" needle if necessary. Sew the neckband seam using the Up through the Bar method.

Fold inwards and sew the band catching each stitch loosely.

Sewing Up

This should be done from the outside using two different techniques Weaving and Up through the Bar.

Sew the sleeve seams including the ribbed bands using the Up through the Bar method. Reinforce the beginning of the cuff.

Sew the remaining shoulder seam first if this is not already done using the Weaving method loosely.

Lay the garment flat and find the armpit by stretching the cast off (bind off) row of the sleeve as deep as possible (at least 28 cms or 11" from the shoulder seam.) Tie the front to the back at this point on both sides of the body.

Side seams

Use the Up through the Bar method for both the ribbed bands and the stocking stitch (stockinette) side seams. Begin at the band and reinforce the first few stitches. Sew up to the ties at the arm pits. Reinforce again.

Setting in the sleeves

Alternate every stitch using the Weaving method for the sleeve and the Up through the Bar method for the body. Stretch the sleeve.

The sleeve stitches and the body rows will not match. Five stitches from the sleeve will match seven rows from the body as with all drop shoulder garments.

Check the inside for any remaining tails and sew these in along their own colours using a large eyed needle.

Alternative Colourways

The background yarns need to be the darkest, the zig zags medium and the flashes the lightest. Alternatives are:

Purple, red and plum mohair zig zags over a deeper plum and brown and olive background with gold flashes.

Orange, gold and hot pink mohair zig zags over red and purple and blue background with lemon flashes.

White, cream and coffee mohair zig zags over deeper coffee, taupe and grey background with apricot and pale pink flashes.

Key Design Elements

The repetition of the the zig zags is important to hold together the random background.

Art Deco

The simple, spaced, repeating pattern constantly moves the eye over the surface of the fabric. The bi-coloured ribbed bands add to the contemporary look.

Yarns Required

M: UNIQUE 12 ply
  (background)
  lilac 513 x 12

A: UNIQUE 12 ply
  black 507 x 3

B: UNIQUE 12 ply
  saxe blue 521 x 2

Needles

5 mm (U.S.#7, U.K.#6)
  needles for the bands,
  cuff and neckband.

6 mm (U.S.#9 or U.K.#4)
  needles for the body.

Tension or Gauge

stocking stitch (stockinette)
17 sts and 22 rows
to l0 cm (4 inches)

Garment size

Width: 60 cm or $23^1/2''$
Total stitches = 100
Length: 70 cm or $27^1/2''$
Total rows = 152

Back

Cast on loosely 90 sts using the band needles in (A). Rib for 2 rows.

Tie on (M) and use both (A) and (M) to work the bi-coloured ribbing as follows:

On the front facing rows do every knit in (M) and every purl in (A). On the reverse side do every knit in (A) and every purl (M). Do every colour change at the back of the work.

Work the bi-coloured rib for 20 rows and then repeat the two rows of black rib.

Change to the body needles and do a purl row increasing to 100 sts evenly across the row.

Cut some 70 cm (28") lengths of black (A) and 50 cm (20") lengths of (B) in advance.

Begin the graph.

All the body background (M) is in stocking stitch knit the front facing rows and purl the wrong side facing rows. (A) is in stocking stitch.

(B) is in garter stitch (knit every row.) It is important

that the first row of (B) on the graph is always worked on a front facing row.

Reading a Graph

One stitch is represented by one square. Read from the bottom right hand corner to the left for the first knit row. Read from left to right for the purl row of stocking stitch even though you will still be knitting from right to

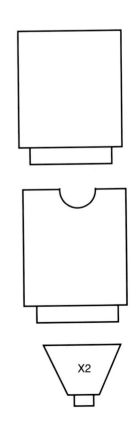

left. Turn the graph upside down if it helps.

Carry behind loosely and connect in the float half way along the (B) rows or use a separate ball of (M) on either side of the images.

The graph repeats 5 times across the body and 8 times up on the back.

There is no armhole shaping for a drop shoulder style and no neck shaping on the back. Cast off (bind off) loosely straight across the last row.

Front

As for the back but this time shape the hole for the neck after working the graph 6 times.

Divide the two shoulders and put the 10 central stitches on a stitch holder or a safety pin. This will make it easier to pick up for the neckband and will help make the neck elastic. Decrease one stitch every 2nd row until 40 sts remain on each shoulder. Continue straight until the front matches the back in length. Cast off (bind off) loosely.

Sleeves

Both sleeves are the same. Cast on 40 stitches using the band needles. Work the band as for the bottom back band. Change to the body needles. Increase on a purl row evenly to 60 stitches using the body needles.

Repeat the graph 3 times across the first row. Increase one stitch each edge every 4th row. Work the extra stitches using part graphs or all in stocking stitch in (M.) Continue until the sleeve is 80 sts across. Stay on the body needles and do one row in black stocking stitch and one row in black rib. Work 6 rows in bi-coloured rib. Finish the sleeve with two rows of black rib. Cast off (bind off) very loosely.

Neck Band

Sew one shoulder seam using the Weaving method. Use straight needles and make a seam (or sew both shoulders and use round needles or four needles.) Using a "band" needle like a crochet hook, (A) coloured

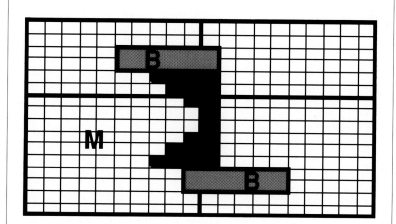

yarn and facing the front of the work knit up stitches evenly around the hole as follows: 20 from the back of the neck, 27 along the curve, knit the 10 from the safety pin to carry the yarn with you, then 27 (Total= 84

stitches.)

To avoid holes in the corners ignore that space and pick up stitches from either side of it.

Rib 2 rows (A), bi-coloured rib for 6 rows and 14 rows of (A.)

Cast off (bind off) very loosely in rib using a "body" needle if necessary. Sew the neckband seam using the Up through the Bar method and the remaining shoulder seam using the Weaving method. Fold the neckband inside. Sew each stitch down to its matching "picked up" stitch but make the loops slightly loose to allow the neck to stretch.

Sewing Up

This should be done from the outside using two different techniques: Weaving and Up through the Bar.

Sew the sleeve seams

115

including the ribbed bands using the Up through the Bar method. Reinforce the beginning of the cuff.

Side seams
Use the Up through the Bar method for both the ribbed bands and the stocking stitch (stockinette) side seams. Begin at the band and reinforce the first few stitches. Sew up to within 28 cms (11") of the shoulder seams. Reinforce again.

Setting in the sleeves
Alternate every stitch using the Weaving method for the sleeve stitches and the Up through the Bar method for the body rows.

Five stitches from the sleeve will match seven rows from the body as with any drop shoulder garment.

Check the inside for any remaining tails and sew these in along the edges of the colour change using a large eyed needle.

Alternative Colourways
Choose a favourite and then work with black and one other detail colour.

A background of saxe blue with a detail of melon

A background of camel with a detail of saxe blue

A background of natural cream with a detail of gold

A background of purple with a detail of gold

A background of gold with a detail of purple

A background of princess blue with a detail of red

Or be more adventurous and play with three colours.

Key Design Element
The relationship between the floating image and the spaces is the key. They are just far enough apart to feel as if they are free form but close enough that they offer the comfort of a repeat.

117

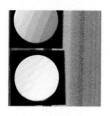

Invent

Patches of delicious yarns in a range of stitches grow from small and intricate to larger and bolder. The colour range is very limited but the odd sparkly or hairy yarn adds to the personality of the fabric. It is a free, "knit as you go and no-pulling-out-allowed" type sweater! By controlling the colours to a very limited range, the whole garment will develop an overall integrity.

Yarns Required

Anything! Ask the person who is to wear it what they want. The best thing is to let them look in your yarn collection and in a yarn store but keep the main "when–in–doubt–use–it" yarn in a favourite darkish colour that knits to around 17 sts to 10 cm (4".) Divide all of your chosen yarn into four and use a bit of everything on each part of the garment. Repeat each colour and pattern at least four times.

Needles

5 mm (U.S.#7, U.K.#6) needles for the bands, cuff and neckband.
6 mm (U.S.#9, U.K.#4) needles for the body.

Tension or Gauge

stocking stitch (stockinette) 17 sts and 22 rows to l0 cm (4 inches)

Garment Size

Width: 52 cm or 20^1/$_2$"
(55 cm or 21^1/$_2$", 58 cm or 23")
Total stitches = 88 (94, 100)
Length: 60 cm or 23^1/$_2$", (70 cm or 27^1/$_2$", 80 cm or 31^1/$_2$")
Total rows = 138 (158, 178)

Back

Using a dark strong yarn cast on loosely 83 (87, 90) sts using 4mm needles. Work the band in rib for 25 rows.

Change to body needles and do a purl row increasing to 88 (94, 100) sts evenly across the row.

Change to body needles.

You are now ready to begin playing in a range of textured stitches.

Make up your own. Use a separate ball for every new colour. Reverse stocking stitch is a good basic texture for an interesting yarn. Moss or seed or any random knit purl stitch will work.

Keep cables to a minimum as they distort the width of

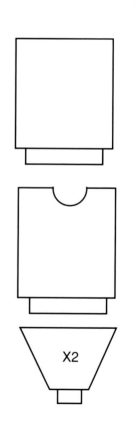

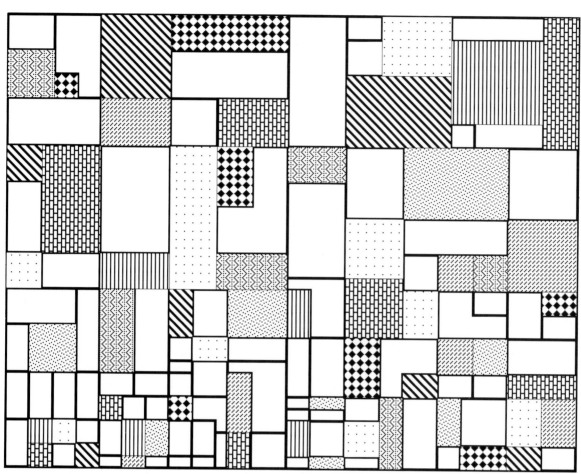

the body but do use them occasionally for a special texture. If half of the stitches are in one colour and the other half are in another colour, the cable will change the direction of the colours.

Hint for Intarsia

When you join in each of the new colours tie a neat knot and leave 10 cm (4 ") tails. Weave these in each stitch at the back while that colour lasts on the graph then leave them till the next row if necessary. If the width of the new colour is too narrow to use this method leave the tail and sew it in later along the edge of the colour change.

Hint for Fairisle

Always work looser than you think you should!

There is no armhole shaping for a drop shoulder style and no neck shaping on the back so continue straight until the back is long enough. You decide. (65 cm or 26" is average.)

Cast off (bind off) straight across the last row loosely so the shoulders will stretch comfortably and use the matching colours for as more professional finish.

Front

As for the back but this time shape the hole for the neck about 10 cm (4") from the

end. Divide the two shoulders by putting the 20 central stitches on a needle holder or a safety pin. This will make it easier to pick up for the neckband and will help make the neck elastic. Decrease one each side every row for 10 rows.

Continue straight for 20 rows or whatever is necessary. Cast off loosely.

Sleeve

The sleeves do not need to be the same colours or the same type of stitch.

Cast on loosely 40 sts using the band needles and band yarn. Rib as for bottom band.

Increase on a purl row to 50 sts. Continue as for the body but also increase one stitch each edge every 4th row . Add in new colours and textures as desired but do not get too carried away in this part as it will end up under the arm. When the sleeve is long enough cast off very loosely. The average sleeve is 50 cm (19^1/2") in length.

Neck Band

Sew one shoulder seam using the Weaving method. Use straight needles and make a seam or sew both shoulders and use round needles or four needles.

Using a "band" needle like a crochet hook and the band yarn or the yarn which matches the top of the garment, face the front of the work and knit up stitches evenly around the hole as follows: 30 from the back of the neck, 15 along the straight vertical edge, 13 along the diagonal, knit the 20 from the safety pin to carry the yarn with you, then 13 and then 15. (Total=106 stitches) To avoid holes in the corners ignore that space and pick up stitches from either side of it.

Work with less stitches if a more fitting neck is required, but not less than 80.

Rib as for the band. Cast off (bind off) very loosely in rib.

Sew the remaining shoulder seam. Sew the band seam using the Up through the Bar method.

To Make Up

This should be done from the outside using two different techniques: Weaving and Up through the Bar.

Sew the sleeve seams including the ribbed bands using the Up through the Bar method. Reinforce the beginning of the cuff. Sew the remaining shoulder seam.

Lay the garment flat and find the armpit by stretching the cast off (bind off) row of the sleeve as deep as possible (at least 28 cms or 11 inches from the shoulder seam.) Tie the front to the back at this point on both sides of the body.

Side seams

Use the Up through the Bar method for both the ribbed bands and the stocking stitch (stockinette) side seams. Begin at the band and reinforce the first few stitches. Sew up to the ties at the arm pits. Reinforce again.

Setting in the sleeves

Alternate every stitch using the Weaving method for the sleeve stitches and the Up through the Bar method for the body rows.

Five stitches from the sleeve

will match seven rows from the body as for any drop shoulder garment.

Check the inside for any remaining tails and sew these in along the edges of the colour change using a large eyed needle.

Alternative Colourways

The original uses black, charcoal and navy with small amounts of camel.

Alternatives could be: black, browns and plums, with small amounts of red

black, blue and forest greens, with small amounts of bright purples

black, purples and reds, with small amounts of gold.

Use more of the brighter or lighter colours up towards the shoulders.

Key Design Elements

The key is the repetition of the yarns and the patterns. These repetitons do not need to be obvious but they are the key to making the apparent randomness work.

The basic division of area is also important. Small blocks growing to large ones provide a sense of scale and planning and also make the shoulders look as if they are stretching the fabric. The base colour which repeats is also part of the structure of the design, regardless of where that yarn appears.

Leading the Eye

Basic Colour Theory

Our response to a sweater is based first on our response to the colours used, then on the design and sometimes on the texture, and then on the shape and fit of the garment.

The total response may only take a split second but even in this split second our response to colour, is first. If a designer or manufacturer wants you to respond to the cut or silhouette first they will use a neutral coloured or black fabric so your eye skips over this step very quickly. If they want you to notice the detailing first they will choose a very light neutral colour. Even if you choose to work with a neutral colour, you must still make that choice.

Unfortunately, choosing colours is the very aspect of thinking independently that worries most knitters. They know what they like and what they don't like but they feel this does not give them a broad enough base to choose well. This is true. Although knowing what

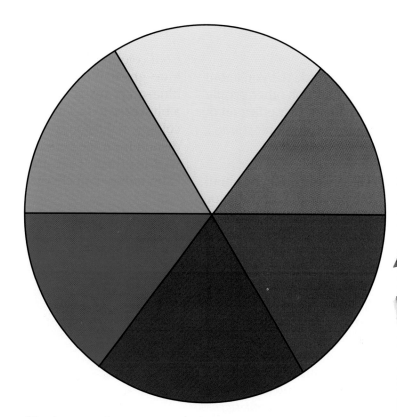

you like is a good start, it is not enough...especially if you are designing for someone else. This is the true test of a designer's skill.

The success of a sweater design will probably be determined by a combination of criteria

Is it flattering to the figure or physique?

Is the colour flattering to the skin tone and eye and hair colour of the wearer?

Do the designs and colours together give the "intended" feeling?

This word "intended" is the key word. A designer "intends" to create a particular feeling or "intends" to resolve problems in a particular way.

If you want the sweater to make you look taller and thinner and reflect your outgoing personality, for example, then you must make colour and design choices with that in mind.

The "choices" you make, and why you make them, are what colour and design theory are all about.

Colour Choices

The following groups of words are key words for colour choices:

These words tell you about their effect on other people and about their effect on the figure or physique: *warm, cool, dark, light.*

These words tell you about the personality of the colour: *clear, intense, grey, muddy.*

These words tell you about the way the colours are made: *primary, secondary, tertiary.*

These words tell you about their mathematical relationships on the color wheel and how to use them together: *monochromatic, analogous, complementary, split complementary.*

Warm colours are yellow, gold, orange, apricot, honey... any colour with a

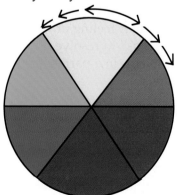

red or gold base to it. These colours make you feel warmer towards the person wearing them. They have more energy particularly if they are clear, bright colours.

They also make the area they are covering look bigger.

Cool colours are blue, blue–green, blue–purple, blue–grey; any colour with a blue base to it. These colours make you feel more distant from the person wearing them. They are calm rather than energetic.

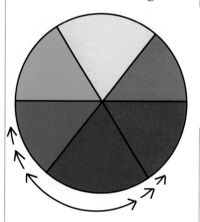

They also make the area they are covering look smaller.

Light colours (tints) are any colours with white added. The eye will see these colours more easily. These colours make the area they are covering look bigger.

Dark colours (shades) are any colour with black added. The eye is less interested in these colours particularly in winter. They make the area they are covering look smaller.

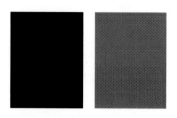

Clear colours are colours that have no mixing or interference. They are fresh and have a quick, light, energetic feel to them.

Intense colours (sometimes called saturated colours) are colours with a lot of dye in them. They are rich and important. They have a feeling of reality and personality to them.

Greyed colours have an aged feeling to them. This suggests a sophistication born of life experience.

122

Muddy colours have an earthy feeling to them. They have a brown, complex base and contain all three primary colours.

Primary colours are red, yellow and blue. They are the "first" colours and they are positioned at the corners of an equal sided triangle on the colour wheel. They have a feeling of youth and energy. They are not complex or experienced. They are great for sporty sweaters or for children.

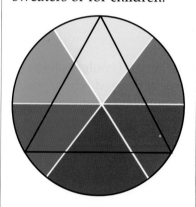

Secondary colours are made of two primary colours mixed together. They are also positioned at the corners of an equal sided triangle on the colour wheel. They still have an energetic feel but they are a little more complex.

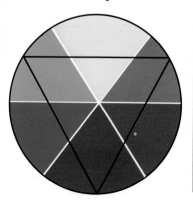

Tertiary colours are positioned in two different places depending on which theory you prefer. They are in between a primary and a secondary colour having more of one than the other in some theories.

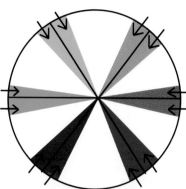

If this is the case then I need another word to explain the position of all those colours not covered so far, which are predominant in baskets of yarn.

I call them *Casserole lid colours*. These are all the colours which have some red *and* some yellow *and* some blue in them. This covers all those complex, mixed yarns which come out of the dye pot when a bit of everything has been thrown in. They are positioned not "on" the colour wheel but "above" it, like a lid.

In a design, they have the effect of slowing down the energy and adding an element of "experience."

Generally children do not like them and they work best with themselves, not mixed with clear bright colours.

Monochromatic colours are in one line on the colour wheel. They are safe to use, particularly if they are also cool. They work best if there are many little steps between the lightest and the darkest. They are also ideal if you wish to change textures and weights of yarn in one garment.

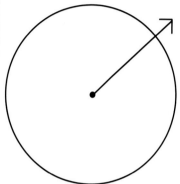

Analogous colours are within 90° of each other on the colour wheel. They are "filler" colours. They broaden the base like a thick paint brush and are richer than using all one colour. If you need more 'physical amounts of yarn' then adding in other analogous colours on the same ring of the colour wheel will be effective. Designing with a soft paint brush and merging colours will encourage you to use analogous colours.

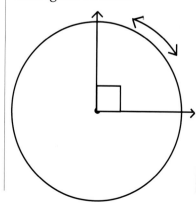

Complementary colours are opposite each other on the colour wheel. They define each other like two people arguing. The difference between them becomes the most important issue. Complementary colours *zap* a design. They also create lines between the colours. You cannot merge gently from one complementary colour to another as you can with analogous colours. To design with complementary colours work with a pen outline and then colour in the areas.

Red and green, orange and blue, and yellow and purple are complimentary colours.

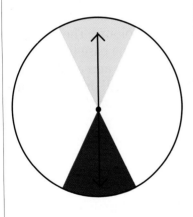

Split complementary colours are complimentary colours with a small difference. Instead of working with the colour which is exactly opposite, a split takes place on one side so three colours are working together. Red will be working with yellow-green and blue-green but not a straight green. Or green will be working with an orange-red and a purple-red but not a straight red. These are like very clever, adversarial conversations. In a sweater, they are a play on colour.

Proportions of Colour

The warmer or lighter a colour, the less is needed to balance a design.

Light yellow and light pink are very powerful, in design. The only colour which will knock them is white.

White is actually the most powerful of all. Yellow is next then orange and lime-green. Red and green are equal although I find most greens tend to feel cooler than the reds. Blue-purple and blue-green are very quiet and blue is the quietest of all. Navy and black are virtually non-existent so they can be used in very large amounts.

Black can be used as a focus in a light design but in a 'cut– out' sense.

Helping the Physique

The lighter and warmer colours should be used where you want to enlarge an area or attract attention e.g. shoulders and up in the vee below the face.

Darker and cooler colours should be used where you do not want attention to settle e.g. the lower half of the body and the outsides of the hips and tummy.

Basic Line Theory

Design involves colour primarily but it also involves division of area and basic line theory.

A sweater front is basically square. It can be divided in many ways.

Our sense of space is effected by the direction the line. A horizontal division will make the body look shorter and wider.

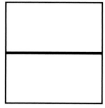

A vertical division will make the body look taller and thinner.

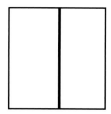

Where we place this line will also have different effects. Straight across the middle or straight up the middle will create a line of symmetry. This central division is very safe but also very predictable.

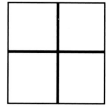

A division of two thirds, by one third is appealing, it has a mathematical base and it is less predictable.

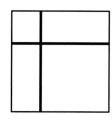

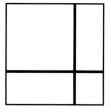

If we choose to decorate each area with different types of lines, each area will have a different area or personality.

Short, sharp, random lines will give a feeling of busy irritation but it will also attract out attention.

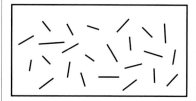

Hard, thick, strong lines in diagonals will give a feeling of definite intentions and direction.

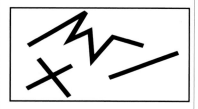

Soft, light, wavy lines will give a feeling of gentle vagueness.

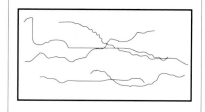

Spots in a repeating design will give a feeling of busy predictability but perhaps also a feeling of entertainment because of their association with children.

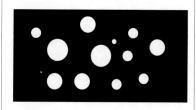

As a basic rule the description of the line also describes the feelings it will give. Try describing your designs and this may tell you what sort feelings others will get from them.

Here is a basic rule you may find helpful when designing.

"Do it once and it is a mistake. Do it twice and it is planned. Do it three times and it is a design." Do it four times and it is boring.

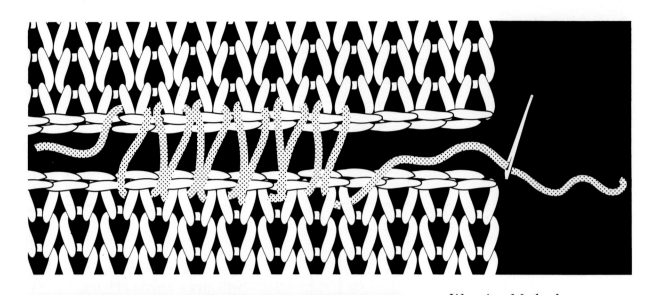

Weaving Method

Up through the Bar Method

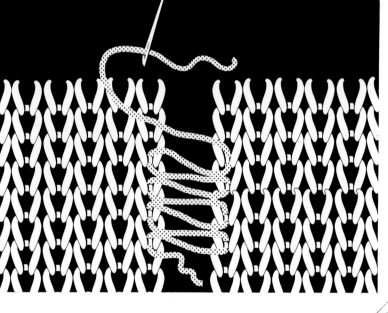

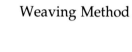

Fairisle

Intarsia

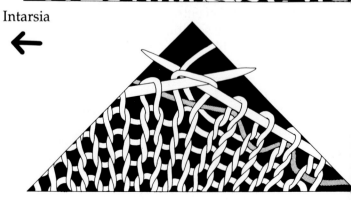

126

Border Art

The borders and polymer jewellery in this book were originally made of coloured polymer clays by Kathleen Amt.

This coloured polymer clay is similar to children's modelling clay but it may be permanently hardened with heat.

Designs or images are produced by laminating different coloured pieces of polymer together so that the graphics are embedded, not painted, on the surface. This technique, called "millefiore" meaning "thousand flowers," came from ancient Egypt, was refined by the Romans, and eventually used in Venitian glass. Strips, sheets and canes of various colours are pressed together to form a larger cane or loaf. The cross-section gives the desired image. A jelly roll cake with its spiral is an example of this technique.

In this book the overall design of each border is a collage of several different millifiore slices applied to a base colour. Once the finished piece has been fired it is durable, lightweight and slightly resilient. These characteristics also make it suitable for jewellery.

For further information on working with polymers please refer to the following book: "The New Clay" by Nan Roche, Publisher Seymour Bress, 1990

Kathleen Amt

Kathleen Amt grew up in the Black Hills of South Dakota, studied at Colorado State University at Fort Collins, and spent 1966-68 as a Peace Corps Volunteer in Thailand.

A love of creating objects led her to pursue a career as artist/teacher in metals, ceramics and fibre. During her sixteen years as an instructor, she was also Director of an Arts and Crafts Centre and, in 1974, a founding member of Fiberworks located in the Torpedo Factory Arts Center, Alexandria, Virginia.

She built and operated a ceramic studio in Woodville, Virginia from 1975 until 1980 when a neck injury caused her to seek other media.

In 1986 she studied and taught at Pyramid Atlantic, a centre for books, prints and paper in Washington D.C. She is currently with Fiberworks at the Torpedo Factory concentrating on books and paper.

Kathleen had worked with coloured porcelains and white polymer during her ceramic studio days but in 1987 was inspired by the work of Kathleen Dustin to use coloured polymer "in" and "on" her books. She is now doing some books completely in coloured polymer including the pages themselves.

Her paperworks and books have been exhibited internationally and are found in private collections and the National Art Library of the Victoria and Albert Museum in London. She is represented by Joshua Heller Rare Books in Washington D.C. Her work is also available through Fiberworks at the Torpedo Factory, Studio 14, 105 N. Union St. Alexandria, VA 22314, U.S.A. Kathleen can be contacted with a stamped self addressed envelope : Kathleen Amt, 4011 30th St. Mt Rainier, MD 20712, U.S.A.

Note from Lee: Kathy, thank you. Polymer may not have been your first choice as a media but I for one am thankful that you turned your attentions to it. I am also thankful that you have a natural desire to experiment and a wonderful sense of humour. It has been a joy to work with you, these past few months as it will be into the future.

Thank you to:

Knitters

Renee Jo Ashby
 Gold Rock
Viola Chou
 Slash and Dash
Paula Hardcastle
 Corporate Spaces
Mary Ann Jackson
 Paw Prints
Elaine Kaplan
 Silk Leaves
Mareen Lasek
 Consistent Cables
Kelly Meyer
 Strata
Nancy Rael
 How I Love Thee
Virginia Mae Smith
 Soft Rock
Judy Whelan
 Nature's Mountain
Jackie Zipf
 Lightening

Models

Puppies for Paw Prints
 Margaret and
 Julie Walton
 13975 Wayside Dr,
 Clarkesville MD 21029
James J. Allman
 Nature's Mountain
 How I Love Thee
 Lightening
 Corporate Spaces
Allison Baritz
 How I Love The
 Outlet
Jamie Dettor
 Cubist Kiss
James Hill
 Outlet
 Cubist Kiss
 Computer Chips
 Santa Fe
Jim Hill
 Side Bar

Michael Houston
 Silk Leaves
 Consistent Cables
 Soft Rock
Charles Kirkland, Jr.
 Giant Cables
André Lee
 Gold Rock
 Parking Lot
Sarah Mesa
 Cubist Kiss
Lisa Perry
 Side Bar
Al Scolnik
 Corporate Spaces
Michele Smith
 Giant Cables
Jamie Starke
 Invent
 Paw Prints
Michael Starke
 Strata

Production

A.K.A. Photographers
 Judy Herrman
 and Michael Starke
 Rockland Arts Center
 Ellicott City, MD 21043
 (301) 461 2786
 for being fun
 photographers and
 emergency models
Dan Talenko, Josephine
 Talenko and Robin
 Roman of Hot Heads Etc
 801 Wayne Ave
 Silver Spring MD 20910
 (301) 585 7070
 for doing Hair-Art and
 Make-over miracles on
 short notice
Kathy Amt for her kindness
 and the borders
Randy Brooks
 for the cover design

Sue Brickell
 of Brickell Graphics
 12201 Howard Lodge
 Sykesville, Md 21784
 (301) 442 5658
 for the layout and
 production
Vernon Dunning of Capital
 Presentations for the
 detailed graphs

Special thanks to:

Joan "Beeker" for saying
 "yes" to every request
Renee Ashby for
 performing above and
 beyond the call of a
 yarn store which
 happens to be:
 Fiberworks
 17800 New Hampshire
 Ashton, MD 20861
 (301) 854 3419
Betty Williams and Donna
 Zalusky for knitting
Carolyn Buckingham for
 bringing me to the U.S
 for the first time
Julia Sant Mire of NZ
 Ray Hill of MD
 Anita Weiss of CA
 Millie Bankhert of Fibre
 Fancy, Clinton NY
Susan Bumbarger of GA
 and Sally Melville of
 Canada for their blind
 faith
Al Scolnik for smiling at
 me on a train between
 New York and
 Washington when I had
 planned to live in New
 Zealand
George and Jinx Vermef
 for making this book
 possible